Psychoanalytic Scholia on the Homeric Epics

Contemporary Psychoanalytic Studies

Editor

Jon Mills

Associate Editors

Gerald J. Gargiulo
Keith Haartman
Ronald C. Naso

Editorial Advisory Board

Howard Bacal, Alan Bass, John Beebe, Martin Bergmann, Christopher Bollas, Mark Bracher, Marcia Cavell, Nancy J. Chodorow, Walter A. Davis, Peter Dews, Muriel Dimen, Michael Eigen, Irene Fast, Bruce Fink, Peter Fonagy, Leo Goldberger, Oren Gozlan, James Grotstein, R.D. Hinshelwood, Otto F. Kernberg, Robert Langs, Joseph Lichtenberg, Nancy McWilliams, Jean Baker Miller, Thomas Ogden, Owen Renik, Joseph Reppen, William J. Richardson, Peter L. Rudnytsky, Martin A. Schulman, David Livingstone Smith, Donnel Stern, Frank Summers, M. Guy Thompson, Wilfried Ver Eecke, Robert S. Wallerstein, Brent Willock, Robert Maxwell Young

VOLUME 20

The titles published in this series are listed at *brill.com/cps*

Psychoanalytic Scholia on the Homeric Epics

By
Konstantinos I. Arvanitakis

BRILL
RODOPI

LEIDEN | BOSTON

Cover illustration: Terracotta vase, attributed to the Berlin Painter, ca. 490 B.C.
The Metropolitan Museum of Art, Fletcher Fund, 1956 (56.171.38). www.metmuseum.org

Library of Congress Cataloging-in-Publication Data

Arvanitakis, Konstantinos I., author.
 Psychoanalytic scholia on the Homeric epics / By Konstantinos I. Arvanitakis.
  pages cm. -- (Contemporary psychoanalytic studies ; volume 20)
 Includes bibliographical references and index.
 ISBN 978-90-420-3927-8 (pbk. : alk. paper) -- ISBN 978-9401212083 (e-book) 1. Homer--Criticism and interpretation. 2. Homer--Knowledge--Psychology. I. Title.

PA4037.A78 2015
883'.01--dc 3

2015008289

This publication has been typeset in the multilingual "Brill" typeface. With over 5,100 characters covering Latin, IPA, Greek, and Cyrillic, this typeface is especially suitable for use in the humanities. For more information, please www.brill.com/brill-typeface

ISSN 1571-4977
ISBN 978-90-420-3927-8 (paperback)
ISBN 978-94-012-1208-3 (e-book)

Copyright 2015 by Koninklijke Brill NV, Leiden, The Netherlands.
Koninklijke Brill NV incorporates the imprints Brill, Brill Hes & De Graaf, Brill Nijhoff, Brill Rodopi and Hotei Publishing.
All rights reserved. No part of this publication may be reproduced, translated, stored in a retrieval system, or transmitted in any form or by any means, electronic, mechanical, photocopying, recording or otherwise, without prior written permission from the publisher.
Authorization to photocopy items for internal or personal use is granted by Koninklijke Brill NV provided that the appropriate fees are paid directly to The Copyright Clearance Center, 222 Rosewood Drive, Suite 910, Danvers, MA 01923, USA.
Fees are subject to change.

This book is printed on acid-free paper.

For Alix and Penelope

Contents

Prologue		1
1	From wrath to ruth	3
	Introduction: of time and mortality	3
	Achilles' metabasis	11
	Epilegomena	18
2	Homer's theory of poetry: Psychoanalytic notes on the primal metaphor	27
	Metaphora	28
	In the court of Scheria	33
	Aoidé	38
	A metaphor of the primal metaphor	45
3	The return of Odysseus: Questions of time, space, and creative discovery	49
	Time, space	53
	Nostalgia and epistemophilia	58
4	The other journey: *Nekyia*	63
5	The tragic in the *Iliad*	79
	The tragic	80
	The tragic in the Iliad	84
	The tragic act	92
	Concluding remarks	96
Epilogue	ον φωνήεν	99
Bibliography		109

Prologue

A psychoanalyst entering the territory of poetry is, admittedly, entering foreign territory. Yet, in listening to his analysand's narratives the analyst enters a world which is no less foreign. The analytic ear *always* listens to the "foreign." And the analyst's interpretations return to the analysand from the foreign Other. Such interventions are always *essays*, tentative forays into a foreign land, and their value lies only in their occasional capacity to re-shuffle the psychic game-board and thereby create a new dynamic.

Of all the arts, poetry is perhaps the art form that can be said to provide a "royal road" to the Unconscious. Hence the temptation of the psychoanalyst to enter into a play with poetry. In the present work, however, unlike most attempts of what has been termed "applied psychoanalysis," the "interpretations" are essentially formulated by the Poet himself rather than by the analyst, who merely follows and tries to understand them and to record them.

Psychoanalysis, since its appearance more than a century ago in the German-speaking world, in a climate richly imbued with the classical spirit, has shown a distinct fascination with classical tragedy and this interest has continued with Freud's followers. The great Homeric Epics, on the other hand, have been remarkably and uniformly neglected as a focus of psychoanalytic attention. It is as if the Homeric Epics belonged more to a prehistoric *pre-oedipal* world which, for a long time, was not the dominant concern of psychoanalysis. But there were other reasons as well. The Great Epics resisted the type of analysis popular in the early days of the discipline, whose principal motive was to provide added support and legitimacy for the psychoanalytic theory of character and conflict. The notion of "character" as we understand it today is difficult to delineate in this early form of poetry. Character emerges and solidifies in the course of time, no less in literature than in the psychological development of the infant. In the Homeric Epics we are dealing with a world in a sort of pre-oedipal psychic flux – the terrain of great poetry – where character is found in *statu nascendi*.

In turning my attention to the Homeric Epics, I must admit and state at the very outset a certain theoretical bias. But, then, is any listening ever "innocent"? Mine is through an ear essentially shaped to be more sensitive to an *object relations* dynamic, but with the fundamental specification – a postulate – that there is a time of being *prior* to any possibility of object relations. This obviously deviates from the Kleinian model. It places the *nucleus* of psychic development and the source of all pathology at the earliest moment (a moment which is to last a lifetime) of *differentiation* of the "I" from the original undifferentiated fusional one-ness of the mother-infant unit. This is the moment of transition from One to Two, a transition that creates the possibility of object relations and their evolution (the so-called paranoid-schizoid and depressive positions). All psychic life can be said to rotate around an axis defined by an incessant back-and-forth movement between differentiation and un-differentiation. As a metaphysical *a priori* the "One—Two" dialectic forms not only the basis of a psychoanalytic metapsychology but, also, the ground of all Western metaphysics.

The analysand lies on the couch for the first time, in the first analytic session, with the analyst out of view. The human paradox in its overwhelming totality is instantly posited, and all begins from here. The analysand is alone and he/she is, also, "face-to-face" with an Other. An invisible Other (the Unconscious, the analyst). Psychic life begins in the presence of an absent object. And so, out comes the first *word*, the first sound. It is close to the body and it is of the nature of an *act*. The years of analysis that will follow will be various attempts to *elaborate* that first physical language. As the primal language of the *infans* and, phylogenetically, of *Homo sapiens*, it is an affirmation of duality and a resolute attempt to overcome it, an agonizing *metaphora* to link with the Other self as an absence, to bridge the existential gap and thereby construct a foundation for Being. It is a metaphor in the literal, not the metaphoric sense, and as such, it is pure poetry.

There is an underlying claim in all this. It is my belief that there is an inner affinity of the psychoanalytic enterprise to poetry, borne through the metaphoric function of the primal word. Psychoanalysis may be much closer to poetry than to neuroscience – a claim that clearly goes against the fashions of the day.

The short essays included in this book form no particular sequence, are autonomous and can be read independently. In the last chapter, an attempt is made to bring together various threads that emerge in my random (?) peregrination through the Homeric Epics. Unstated though apparent in this work is my pre-verbal, so to speak, love for "Homer" – a psychoanalyst's love for a forever elusive and never-knowable object.

Chapter One

From wrath to ruth

> *Remember me in after time, whenever anyone of men on earth, a stranger who has seen and suffered much, comes here and asks of you: 'Who think ye, girls, is the sweetest singer that comes here, and in whom do you most delight?' Then answer, each and all, with one voice: 'He is a blind man, and dwells in rocky Chios: his lays are evermore supreme.'*
> Homeric Hymn to Apollo (West, 2003)

INTRODUCTION: OF TIME AND MORTALITY

More than two-and-a-half-thousand years ago the "blind bard" composed, in meter, the folktales that came to be known as the Homeric Epics. Recently, over the past two years alone, five new English translations of the *Iliad* have appeared (Lattimore, 2011; Mitchell, 2011; Muirden, 2012; Verity, 2011; Whitaker, 2012), prompting the airing of a BBC panel of academics to discuss the seemingly unabated interest in the Poem. Unavoidably the question arises: What is the basis of the continued appeal of these Ancient epics in a world which is so drastically changed since the time of their first appearance? Such an inquiry is likely to lead us to some fundamental (and, despite appearances, so far unchanged) principles of functioning of the human psyche. That would explain the persisting modernity of Homer. It is the aim of this chapter to explore this question by focusing on the *Iliad*.

Homer, who probably lived in the eighth century BCE, occupied a central role in the *paedeia* of classical times and his influence subsequently extended diachronically to the entire Western world. Plato attests to the fact that he was "the educator of all Hellas" and that he was studied for guidance in the conduct of life (*Rep.* 606e). Plato further considers Homer "the original teacher and master of tragic poets" (*Rep.* 595c). But there were, also, well-voiced criticisms of his message. For instance, Xenophanes, already in the sixth century BCE, denounced the human immorality that Homer attributed to gods (Kirk & Raven, 1971, p. 168) and, more importantly, Plato himself condemned Homer's, and poetry's in general, illusory representation of reality (*Rep.* 595a-608c). However, it is beyond question that, through their profound influence on the Greek mind, the Homeric Epics became the source and foundation of Western aesthetics, ethics and metaphysics. The unifying Greek thought, always in search of "first principles" which could give a systematic and comprehensive account of reality as a structurally harmonious unity, tended to integrate the Beautiful, the Good, and the True into one fundamental entity: Being. Thus, in the Greek mind, there was no distinction as such between the aesthetically pleasing work of art, the ethically just action, and knowledge of truth. All of these were thought to be expressed in various ways in the Homeric Epics. In particular, Homer's pivotal role in the origin of that uniquely Greek and Western form of art, tragedy, is to be noted. What is articulated for the first time in the Epics is the primordial opposition between human Will and impersonal Fate. The *men...de* antinomy, deeply characteristic of Greek thought and the basis of all philosophical and political dialogue, finds its origin here.[1] Human conflict, constitutive of the Western psyche, will become from now on the signpost of our collective consciousness. Hence Jaeger's (1973) assertion that Homer, beyond being the creator and shaper of Greek life and of the Greek character, "became the teacher of all humanity."

The *Iliad* is a long poem of approximately fifteen-thousand-six-hundred lines composed in dactylic hexameters. It was subdivided, probably during Hellenistic times, into twenty-four Books following the letters of the Greek alphabet. It narrates a brief episode of fifty-one-days' duration at the beginning of the tenth year of the Trojan War. The action falls roughly into three parts: Books 1-9, 11-18, and 19-24: a three-movement composition which presumably could permit recitation over three days.[2] The divine Muse, daughter of the goddess *Mnemosyne* (Remembrance), is evoked to tell of the wrath of Achilles and its disastrous consequences.[3] The tone is majestic and the introduction of time reversals at the very outset (prospective—retrospective) effectively elevates the significance of the events to be recounted onto a higher level, outside the constraints of linear time, investing them with a tragic import. The very narration of these deeds appears as a necessary act in the chain of events dictated by Moira.

We are in the tenth year of the War. The camp of the Achaeans, outside the besieged city of Ilium, is being decimated by a plague sent by Apollo as punishment for the disrespect shown his priest by King Agamemnon: Agamemnon holds the priest's daughter, Chryseis, as his share of the booty and refuses to accept her father's ransom. When he is eventually persuaded to let her free to return to her father so that Apollo is appeased, Agamemnon seizes as a recompense Achilles' share, the maiden Briseis. In the violent quarrel that breaks out between Achilles and Agamemnon, Achilles barely restrains himself,

---

[1] The *men...de* construction indicates contrasting perspectives or views of reality.

[2] Book X, an interlude, is probably a later addition.

[3] It should be noted that to the Homeric mind what the Muse narrates through the voice of the poet-bard are recollections of true events. See, for example, *Odyssey* 8: 487-98, and *Iliad* II: 485.

with the help of Athena, from killing the king. Dishonored and humiliated, Achilles angrily now withdraws from battle and appeals through his mother to a consenting Zeus to avenge him by punishing the Achaeans. Thus the tide turns against the Achaeans, notwithstanding their valiant efforts to resist the Trojans' onslaught led by the brave Hektor. Agamemnon, in despair, sends ambassadors to Achilles, offering him handsome amends if he agrees to return to battle, but Achilles, after receiving the ambassadors with kindness, refuses to yield. He questions the value of life heroically lived but short, as opposed to eschewing death and returning home to live a comfortable long life.

With the break of dawn of the third day the Great Battle begins. Blind hatred and strife now reign supreme. The Achaeans suffer even greater reverses, their chieftains are all wounded one by one and the troops are pushed back to their ships. At this point Achilles begins to relent and yields to Patroklos' plea to let *him* enter the battle wearing Achilles' armor so that the Trojans will take him for Achilles and flee. Patroklos' ambition and unrestrained fighting ebullience, however, will cost him his life at the hands of Hektor, who will then strip him of Achilles' armor and put it on himself. The grief of Achilles at the loss of his friend is profound as he bemoans "Oh, would that Strife and Rage perish!" A splendid new armor is made for him by the smith-god Hephaistos and Achilles now enters the battlefield himself in savage fury determined to take revenge for Patroklos' death. Even the gods now enter the fighting, and the entire cosmic order is disturbed. Water and Fire are at war with each other, and Scamander, a river of life, is turned into a river of death. Achilles slays Hektor and viciously drags his corpse behind his chariot. He knows his own end by the Skaean Gates is now near. Mourning scenes become dominant: Achilles is mourning Patroklos, Achilles' mother Thetis mourns her son's imminent death, and Hektor's old parents, wife and also Helen – who had been the origin of this war – mourn brave Hektor.

Old king Priam sets out to ransom his son's body, which Achilles, in his unremitting grief, still drags around Patroklos' grave. Priam arrives at Achilles' Gate as if to the Gate of the House of the Dead. But now face-to-face, the two mortal enemies gaze at each other in awe and in marvel. This is the climactic "awe-some" moment of Aristotelian *anagnorisis* that brings about a transformation, "a change from ignorance to knowledge, either towards friendship or enmity," in the words of Aristotle. Tragic action, Aristotle tells us, is to have gravity and magnitude (*Poetics* 1449b 24-25). What do Achilles and Priam recognize in themselves and in each other at that moment? Who is the Achilles who now lifts gently with his own hands Hektor's washed and anointed body onto a bier, thereby commencing *himself* Hektor's funeral rites? Hektor of the flashing helmet.

> *For on this wise have the gods spun the thread for wretched mortals*
> (Homer, 1920, *Iliad*, XXIV: 525)[4].

---

[4] Translations of Homer (1920), *Homeri Opera* are by the author.

Such poetry – like all great poetry – is profoundly disturbing. It inspired a wave of aesthetic and moral skepticism in the Ancients who questioned the worldview presented therein. Centuries later, M. l'abbé d'Aubignac (1604-1676) had a solution: Homer never really existed! The Epics, d'Aubignac held, exhibit such poor style, base morality, and multiple inconsistencies in the narration of the story that they are surely a mere compilation of a number of lays clumsily patched together by some unskilled assembler .

And so the seed was sown for the great nineteenth century debate known as "The Homeric Question" which dominated the scene of Homeric studies for over a century and a half. It was a philological obsession in line with the historicism of the times and aided by the romantic spirit which exulted in a poem arising spontaneously from the collective soul of the people, without the intervention of an individual creator-poet. The scholars' concern was exclusively the manner of composition of the Epics. They scrutinized the text with their analytic instruments in search of clues of its origin and evolution, pushing aside all literary considerations of the poems themselves and of the art of their creator. The focus was on the mechanics of composition alone. The field soon became sharply divided and a passionate academic war started between two camps: the "Analysts" and the "Unitarians." The major work that inaugurated the "analytic" approach was Friedrich August Wolf's *Prolegomena ad Homerum*, which appeared in 1795. Wolf argued that the epics could not be the work "of a single genius, burst forth suddenly from the darkness in all their brilliance, just as they are." He believed that they were composed orally, without the help of writing, by various poets, who transmitted them in oral recitation for many generations while introducing all along, deliberately or accidentally, many changes, until the poems were finally written down in the 6th century BCE (in what is known as the Peisistratian recension). But even after this there were further modifications brought about in the attempts of various "editors" to polish and streamline the assembled corpus. An artistic structure was attained but that was not the creation of a single great poet; instead, it was the result of the collective effort of many. The Epics as we know them are, therefore, according to Wolf's view, the product of an evolution, and this explains certain inconsistencies in the narrative, language or social customs which were noted even by the Ancients.

This serious challenge to the authorship of Homer was bound to produce an immediate and passionate reaction. Schiller spoke of the literary "barbarism" of such analyses (Schmitz, 2007, Letter to Goethe dated 27 April 1798). The analytical approach, in challenging the unity of the poet, was in effect seriously calling into question the very unity and aesthetic merit of the poems themselves. More than a century later, Milman Parry's and Albert Lord's theory of oral composition, based on their work on the *Iliad* and on Serbo-Croatian heroic songs, added tangible support from the field of comparative literature to the old assemblist theory of the *Liederjäger* (the "lay-hunters," as the analysts were called at the time) (Parry, 1971; Parry & Lord, 1954). But, back in the nineteenth century, the "unitarian" response to the analysts was not slow in making its appearance. G. W. Nitzsch, in a number of books (Nitzsch, 1841, 1852), studying the overall plan of the *Iliad*, argued for a single poetic genius who, although drawing from earlier songs, surpassed his predecessors and created a masterpiece of enduring power. Nitzsch's work was an influential refutation of the Wolfian hypothesis and it strengthened considerably the approach of the unitarian camp. A serious blow to the analysts in the twentieth century was W. Schadewaldt's *Iliastudien* (first published in 1938 in Leipsig)[5] and this prepared the ground for the most recent version of the unitarian view, the so-called "neoanalyst hypothesis." The neoanalysts, whose chief spokesman is Kakridis, use analytic textual techniques in search of earlier pre-Homeric narrative elements in Homer's poetry, which, however, they believe were utilized and adapted by one great poet who created the *Iliad*, virtually in the form we have it today (Kakridis, 1944; Pestalozzi, 1945). It is worth noting at this juncture that Parry and Lord's (1954) oral poetry theory is not inconsistent with the neoanalytic model and can easily be integrated with it. The significant difference of the neoanalytic approach lies in the poetic magnitude and novelty ascribed by its proponents to a single author-integrator of a final definitive epic, which, they are also inclined to believe, was composed with the help of writing. It can be recalled that Aristotle's views on the Great Epics were unitarian. Aristotle considered as Homer's unsurpassed merit his ability to "weave [the Epics] around one action" (*Poetics* 1451a 28-30), "whole and complete," so that, unlike other epics, "it can be made into one tragedy, or two at the most" (*Poetics* 1459b 3). Aristotle clearly believed Homer to have been the sole author of the Epics.

The Homeric Question and all the passionate polarized argumentation that it generated, dominating Homeric studies as it did for several generations of scholars, turned out to be a most fertile intellectual stimulus leading to the establishment of the distinct discipline of *Altertumswissenschaft* that flourished in the German-speaking world in the nineteenth century. Homer, "the teacher of all humanity," stimulated, once again, studies in Ancient history, linguistics, anthropology, sociology, religion, mythology, and so forth. In time, the extreme polarization of the debate subsided, as the two sides moved, as we saw, more towards the center. The new, in effect, synthetic approach viewed Homer as a superbly gifted innovator who, while steeply embedded in the cultural and spiritual climate of his times and nourished by a rich oral tradition of popular lays and myths as well as traditional narrative styles, themes, type-scenes, formulae, and so forth, used all of these and transformed them in a singular achievement of creating a new poetic masterpiece of timeless human value. Rather than being subservient to his tradition, Homer brought the traditional poetic elements available to him to the service of his art.

---

[5] A third edition of the book was published in Darmstadt in 1966.

For more than a century and a half, however, the poems themselves, their content and literary aesthetic fabric, had been neglected in favor of considerations of the mode of their composition. Without denying the rich yield of such an enterprise, the tide seems to be now turning (de Jong, 1995). Our study here, pursuing a different avenue, that of psychological analysis of the content, will attempt to demonstrate that there is a remarkable *psychological coherence* and a tight psychological cohesiveness in the *Iliad*, and will thus lend further support to the notion that such a work could only have been the creation of one mind of poetic genius, a mind endowed with diachronic radiance.

The Poem called *The Song of Ilium* (Ιλιας ωδη = *Iliad*)[6] was probably given that name in later times. Yet it is not about the war of Troy, even though in the brief episode recounted the larger context of the war is skillfully brought in. From that perspective, Agamemnon's taking away Chryseis, the priest's daughter, at the beginning of the narration, and later forcefully taking Briseis away from Achilles, echoes Paris' abduction of Helen from Menelaos' palace in Sparta, which was the reason for the war. But behind the surface structure of the Trojan conflict, the poet is telling the human story of the root of all wars. The first word that opens the long narrative is *Μηνιν*... The poem is not about Ilium, it is not even about Achilles, an *Achilleis*, as some have thought (Geddes, 1878; Pestalozzi, 1945), in the sense that the *Odyssey* is about Odysseus.[7] It is about *μηνις*: blind rage, unthinkable human cruelty, arrogance, and illusion (*ατη*); it is a *Meniad*. Various lays of the glorious Trojan campaign (which took place about 500 years before Homer's age), of the heroic feats of the Greeks of old, of the Fall of the great City, and so forth, were a prominent element in the cultural climate of the 8th century. But Homer chose, and most likely introduced, a novel and narrower focus: "The Wrath, sing, Oh goddess ..." Kakridis (1985) believes that Homer innovated in narrating a battle in which the Greeks were *defeated*, and it was for that reason that he introduced the theme of Achilles' rage and his consequent withdrawal from battle that accounted for their defeat. I am inclined to believe that Homer specifically focused on rage as a primitive force in order to poetically follow its consequences and its evolution towards compassion and humane feeling. Such a transformation is achieved in Bk XXIV, which, for Lesky (1966), represents "the culmination of the *Iliad* and the starting point of the Western conception of humanity" (p. 39). The two sides of Achilles' character, his "two poles" of anger and gentleness and their interaction, have been noted by a number of authors (Bowra, 1930; Schadewaldt, 1938; Whitman, 1958) and have been considered by some (Bethe, 1914; Wilamowitz-Möllendorf, 1920) as evidence of structural discontinuity and hence of multiple authorship. Wilamowitz-Möllendorf (1920), for example, believed Bk XXIV to be a later addition, and Kirk (1976) finds the Achilles—Priam reconciliation scene in Bk XXIV "unnerving" because it does not fit the heroic *ethos* and code. Yet, Kirk (1976) considers Bk XXIV to be "especially

---

[6] Ilium is Troy.
[7] Thus, contrast the *Odyssey*'s opening: "Of the man, tell me, Oh Muse..."

Homeric," as does Kakridis (1985), its occasional Odyssean phraseology reflecting only a post-Homeric revision. We do believe, on psychological grounds, that the *Iliad*'s last Book is an integral part of what is a unified poetic project and that this Book constitutes precisely what gives the Poem its organic unity, emotional coherence, and profound aesthetic impact.

It has been remarked that the Homeric Epics contain narrative themes and patterns which are also found in the traditional oral story-telling of diverse cultures (Europe, Central Asia, India, etc.), from Antiquity to the present time (Hansen, 1997). Their affinity to Near-Eastern literature is of particular interest.[8] But it has also been noted that this universality of themes applies mostly to the *Odyssey*, which is a typical *nostos* story (cf. for example, The Homecoming Husband, The Identity Test, The Sailor and The Oar, The Ogre Blinded, No-man, etc.). The *Iliad*, by contrast, does not appear to be a variant of a story pattern and is quite specific in its overall structure (the presence of formulaic elements, such as type-scenes, stock expressions and similes, notwithstanding). It develops its unique, well-circumscribed theme of rage and follows it through its multiple manifestations to its transformation in Bk XXIV. The last Book is indispensable to the aesthetic unity of the Poem. We *could* imagine a Homer who would end his Song with Achilles' victory over Hektor (and hence over Troy) and with the mourning of Patroklos. The heroic ideal has been fulfilled, the Achaeans have paid for their hybris against Apollo, and the tragic dimension has been introduced through the now inevitable downfall of the hero, demi-god though he was, since the human dilemma can only be resolved in death. It would have been a great poem even without the final scene. But Homer did not end it there. It is the final scene of the *Poem of Μηνις* which makes it an immortal Poem and secures its place in world literature.[9]

In 1932, Myres drew attention to a striking parallelism in the narrative structure of the opening and of the closing sections of the *Iliad*. This was later studied in great detail by Whitman (1958), who was able to show that the entire structure of the *Iliad* exhibits an architectural symmetry of remarkable precision. "Ring composition," which had been invoked in the narration of single episodes and scenes of the *Iliad*, was now shown to govern the composition of the epic as a whole. This grand design consists of a center, a central point in the narration, which Whitman locates in the Great Battle (Bks XI-XV), with concentric circles spreading outwards, coupling corresponding Books symmetrically on either side of the center. The correspondence is through similarity or antithesis, and it is most striking at the periphery: Books I and XXIV display an almost perfect

---

[8] Sumerian (*Gilgamesh*), Akkadian (*Atrahasis*), Babylonian (*Enuma Elis*), Hebrew (*The Old Testament*), and so on. See Morris (1997).

[9] It is thought likely by some (e.g., Wilamowitz-Möllendorf, 1920, pp. 92-115) that a pre-Homeric version of the story existed which ended with the mutilation of Hektor's body by Achilles, which Achilles only *threatens* to do in our *Iliad* (XXII: 347). Bowra (1962) believes that Homer surprised his audiences by changing the familiar end, making Achilles relent and thereby allowing for a healing of the wrath (p. 55).

balance, based on a *hysteron-proteron* sequence of events (a..b..c—c..b..a). Whitman relates this distinct pattern of composition to the visual symmetry that characterizes geometric art which was prevalent in Homer's time (e.g., Dipylon vases). At a time of geographic expansion and profound social upheavals, art expressed a desire for balance and order. But in the case of oral-aural art, such a structural scheme serves to heighten the dramatic impact of narration. I believe that the center of the composition can be located with precision in XI: 3-14. It is here that "dreadful Strife" descends on the battlefield, uttering her "terrible shrill cry of war" and reigning supreme from now on. This will lead to a cosmic conflict involving gods and men and threatening to "cleave the earth ... and lay bare the ghastly houses of the dead" (XX: 63-65).

The outermost and the sharpest limits of the Poem's frame are the First and the Last Book. It is in the correspondence, most powerfully in the antithetical correspondence between these two Books, as they rotate around the center of "overpowering Strife" of Book XI, that the poet achieves a masterly, almost sculptural, development of his theme. Book One opens with a background of the plague and the funeral pyres in the Greek camp. The Last Book ends with Hektor's funeral in Troy. In Book One, a father's plea (Chrysis) for his daughter has been denied. In Book Twenty-four, a father's plea (Priam) for his son's body is granted. In Book I, Achilles via Thetis makes an appeal to Zeus. In XXIV, Zeus via Thetis makes an appeal to Achilles. In I, the appeal is for revenge. In XXIV, it is for relenting. The quarrel of allies (Agamemnon—Achilles) of Book I reappears, in Book XXIV, but this time as a reconciliation of enemies (Achilles—Priam).

Such balanced contrasts (cf. Herakleitos, in Kirk & Raven, 1971, Fr. 212) delineate the principal axis of a well-defined psychological movement and powerfully underline Homer's dominant theme: the evolution from wrath to ruth.[10] It would, indeed, be difficult to imagine how a poetic project of such breadth and at the same time specificity could be so harmoniously executed and so carefully crafted other than by one superior *aiodos*.

I shall focus on the remarkable change in the character of Achilles in *Iliad*'s last Book (XXIV), his *metabasis* (Aristotle, *Poetics* 1452a 16-18), and reflect on what this change consists of and on how and why it takes place. I shall argue that, through the hero's integration of time, the status – precarious and fluctuating though it may be – of a "whole object" (Klein)/"whole subject" (Heidegger) was attained, and that this gave rise to his capacity for compassion and care. I shall, in the course of the discussion, propose a hypothesis on the origin of our sense of time. Restricting my focus thus, I shall not be commenting on various libidinal issues and oedipal themes present in the *Iliad*.

I suggest that it is the skillful poetic crafting of the dynamic interaction between such universal themes as cruelty and compassion, mortality and a well-rounded view of reality that explain Homer's continuing appeal and his persisting modernity.

---

[10] Ruth is a Middle English word meaning "compassion," still used in *ruthless*.

ACHILLES' *METABASIS*

It has, all along, been a story of unrelenting cruelty and unthinkable horror: Achilles is "nowise soft of heart or gentle of mind but exceedingly fierce" (XX: 467-8), like a lion or a wolf (XXII: 262-3), ready to "carve [Hektor's] flesh and eat it raw" (XXII: 347), "his brute force and wild spirit ... swooping down on the flocks of men to seize his savage feast. He has lost all pity and shame" (XXIV: 42-4). To the dying Hektor, imploring him to accept his parents' ransom and return his body for a decent burial, Achilles retorts:

> *There lives no man who would keep away the dogs from your head, not even if they should bring here and weigh out ransom ten-fold or twenty-fold, and promise even more. Not even if Dardanian Priam were to pay your weight in gold ... Dogs and birds shall devour you whole* (XXII: 348-52).

We thus understand Hekabe's plea in XXIV when she tries to dissuade Priam from going to see Achilles in order to plead for Hektor's body: "He is so savage and faithless a man that he will feel neither pity nor reverence for you" (XXIV: 207-8).

But the old man will not be dissuaded. He goes to Achilles, kneels before him kissing "those terrible man-slaying hands that had slain his many sons." Achilles is astounded:

> *Awestruck – like those overwhelmed by dread as they look upon a man who, possessed by dark blindness, has slain someone in his own country and has now fled to a land of strangers, to the house of a wealthy man* (XXIV: 480-4).

The verb used here for "awe" is θαμβεειν.[11]

Priam speaks of his sorrows, the sufferings he has endured like no other man on the face of the earth, and reminds Achilles of his father. And now something unexpected happens: the fierce warrior, "whose heart is as unbending as iron," gently touches the old man's hand moving him back (XXIV: 508ff). An overpowering wave of grief overtakes both of them as they lament what is forever lost, the sound of their moaning going through the entire encampment. Achilles, filled with pity (οικτειρων) for the white-haired old king, raises him by his hand and sits him upon a chair: "Ah, unhappy man, how many are the evils that you have endured in your heart!" (XXIV: 515-8). He thinks of his own father who was denied an offspring of princely sons, "his only son doomed to an untimely death ... here, far away from my own country, a woe to you and to your children," (XXIV: 542) he tells Priam.

---

[11] θαμβεειν means to be struck with wonder, astonishment, or awe, but in this context also contains an element of dread.

Although Achilles' fiery temper can still be easily aroused (XXIV: 568-70), something has radically changed in the nature of this man. He orders the servants to bathe and anoint Hektor's body and then he, himself, lifts the dead Hektor and lays him on a bier. He then invites Priam to a ritual supper. When the drinking and eating are finished, the two men gaze at each other with marvel and admiration, feeling joy (ταρπησαν) in each other's countenance (XXIV:628-33). The verb used here to indicate "marvel" is θαυμαζειν. Dread (482) has given way to joyful wonderment.

So what exactly has happened at that meeting of the two enemies? The unexpected reversal in Achilles' character is nothing short of a *peripeteia* (περιπετεια) in Aristotle's sense (*Poetics* 1452a 22-29). That this is something out of the ordinary does not escape Achilles himself who knows that if the other Achaeans were to learn about his changed attitude, Priam would be in grave danger, and so, concerned about the old man's safety, he takes measures to protect him.

Let us look back and follow the evolution of events from the beginning.

When Briseis was taken away from Achilles by a man stronger than himself (Agamemnon), Achilles' inflated narcissism was deeply wounded. He could not tolerate such humiliation, shamed in front of the entire Achaean army as he was. Although not the Commander of the expedition, he was after all a demi-god, the son of immortal Thetis. Irreconcilable, unable to accept compromises, at a moment of impulsive narcissistic rage he almost murders Agamemnon. Personal honor was the cornerstone of the heroic code stringently adhered to by himself and his peers, and Achilles' honor is seriously injured at this point. He withdraws from battle, but, although he distances himself from the group, he remains firmly embedded in the conventional group codes of conduct and will remain so until the events of the last Book. We shall return to this point. Achilles' omnipotent, megalomanic vision of himself is apparent in XVI: 97-100. He tells Patroklos: "Would to Father Zeus and Athena and Apollo that, of all the Trojans, not one might escape death, not one of the Argives either, and that we two might escape destruction so that we, alone, might loosen Troy's sacred diadem of towers." Patroklos, we note, is like a twin brother to Achilles, his double, an inseparable part of himself, and this is reflected in XXIII: 83-4 and 126 where their ashes are to be mixed, and Achilles is preparing a great funerary mound for both of them. Further, Achilles' idealized self-image is clearly seen in the Embassy episode (IX), where he proudly rejects Agamemnon's generous offer of reconciliation, saying "I have not the least need for such an honor, for I consider that I have been honored by the disposal of Zeus himself!" (607-8). Such an inflated self-image stems from a state of mind which, in the Homeric world, was attributed to *Ate*, a sort of psychological blindness, an illusion that was believed to be the cause of all evil and destruction. It is *Ate* which is responsible for Agamemnon's arrogant treatment of Apollo's priest, as it will be the cause of Patroklos' death, and equally of the death of Hektor who refused Polydamas' repeated wise counsel. *Ate* and blind rage are above all what determine most of Achilles' actions. The dying Hektor will warn him: "Reflect now" (φραζεο) on your own demise by Paris and Apollo at the Skaean Gates (XXII: 358-60). The verb φραζω here alludes to an earlier scene involving Diomedes who, showing no restraint in fighting even gods, was admonished by Apollo in the following words: "Reflect now, son of Tydeus, and pull back. Do not believe yourself to be equal to gods since never is the race of immortal gods equal to that of men who walk on earth" (V: 440-2). *Ate* generates blind arrogance.

Achilles has been told that his life would be short. Already at the beginning, in I: 352, he calls himself "born to a brief span of life." "Many times had he been told, in confidence, by his mother" that he was not to sack Troy (XVII: 407-8), which would only fall after his death. Thetis, shedding tears, declares to him that he is "doomed to a speedy death, wretched above all men" (I: 417). Temporality is a prominent background to the entire narrative of epic action. But, we must ask, is Achilles blinded by *Ate* regarding the preordained shortness of his life? It is far from clear – at least there is no indication – that he truly realizes or fully comprehends, early in the story, the significance of this truth about his inescapable destiny. That he does not is suggested, for instance, by his response to Agamemnon's ambassadors in IX: He considers himself in position to *choose* between fighting the Trojans and gaining "imperishable renown" but never returning home, or returning to his dear native land, to a long, comfortable life, but losing his glorious renown. *Kleos* vs. *Nostos*. He vacillates. "No raiding and no trading (bought by rich gifts) can bring back a man's breath of life once it has gone through his teeth," (408-9) he asserts. No, tomorrow, at early dawn, he will sail back to the rich soil of Phthia and put off death (his withdrawal will arrest the flow of time). That is his choice!

All would be settled, then, at this point, except... When the ambassadors arrived, they found him "delighting his soul (τερπομενον) with a clear-toned lyre as he sang of the glorious deeds (κλεα) of men" (186-9). It seems that his choice had *already* been made and was the opposite of what he was to declare later to the ambassadors.

Achilles is the only hero in the Homeric Epics who appears as a bard. This unusual image of Achilles (who, only a few lines earlier and later in the same Book, is described as "hard and unrelenting like Death," and also as "cruel, without pity, of an obdurate and evil heart") indicates that we are to expect unexpected developments as the story unfolds. Achilles is clearly a most complex character.

Thus we arrive at Book XI. Achilles has been absent from the narrative scene so far: more than two weeks after the insult he stubbornly stays away from the battlefield, unmoved by the heavy losses of his comrades. We are, here, at what can be considered as the nucleus of the concentric compositional architectonic of the Epic. Deadly Strife is the sole Ruler and "exults with wild groans" at the sight of warriors "raging like wolves" (72-3). It is at this point that Achilles reappears on the scene ending his withdrawal. He has been watching the battle from afar, standing by the stern of his ship. He sees that a man has been wounded and is being carried away. He calls out Patroklos who was inside the hut: "And this was the beginning of Patroklos' doom," we are told mysteriously by the Poet (604). It is, also, the beginning of Achilles' *metabasis*. Achilles is interested to know who the wounded man is and sends Patroklos to the battleground to find out. The old king Nestor, full of surprise, exclaims: "How in the world is it possible that Achilles is now showing compassion for all the sons of Achaeans smitten by arrows?" (656-7). This is the *turning point* of the entire dramatic action. It is as if a line has been irreversibly crossed by the hero at this point, as the result of a free individual act whose consequences will now follow by necessity. The rest of the narrative meticulously traces the unfolding of this chain of events. As foreshadowed here, Achilles will send Patroklos to the battlefield to take part in the battle, in XVI. What we have here is the first instance, the first sign of *concern* on the part of Achilles whose aloofness and arrogance seem to be softened. Caring, to be sure, is expressed explicitly only through the voice of Patroklos who seems to represent Achilles' human, compassionate self. Thus, meeting a wounded Achaean, on his way back, Patroklos is overwhelmed with grief and pity for the man and for all the others destined to die "away from home and friends, glutting with [their] white fat the swift dogs of Troy" (817-8). He employs Achilles' own medical art, the skill that Achilles had learned from the Centaur Chiron, to tend to the wounded man: "And the blood ceased to flow" (848). Attempts at *reparation* (Melanie Klein) make, here, their first appearance.

The unassailable reign of *time* and its unstoppable flow are now powerfully brought into the story through the narrative technique of *prolepsis* (flash-forward). The hordes of men go on fighting for now, we are told, but the wide wall and the trench built by the Achaeans to protect them is not to last long. The bravest of the Trojans will fall, many of the Achaeans also; the city of Priam will be sacked in the tenth year, the surviving Argives will set sail for their dear native land. And then the gods will raze to the ground the works of man. The great wall will be swept away into the salted sea by all the rivers that flow from the mountains of Ida – the rivers on whose banks a race of "men half-divine" had fought and fallen.[12] And the long beach will, once again, be made smooth, covering everything with thick sand. No trace left for the generations to come (XII: 3-35). Except the Song.[13]

But for now Patroklos, deeply affected by the sufferings of the Achaeans, will plead with Achilles to let *him* enter the battle wearing Achilles' armor so that the Trojans will *take him for Achilles* and retreat. Unlike his earlier negative reaction to the ambassadors, Achilles now yields. Regarding his feud with Agamemnon he says: "Let us leave these things be as having gone their way. I was not to be filled with anger forever" (XVI: 60-1). Time is to be unleashed and events are thereby set in motion irreversibly leading to dramatic

---

[12] This is the only instance where Homer uses the epithet "demigods" for humans.

[13] See VI: 357-8: "Zeus brought on us evil doom that in aftertime we may become a song for men that are yet to be."

changes. A characteristic gesture of Achilles' at this point expresses his highly charged emotional state at that moment as he decides to move forward, to act: He *slaps his thighs*, as he urges Patroklos to get up, strap on his (Achilles') armor and prepare for battle. The same gesture had been made earlier by Patroklos (XV: 397) when he had decided to go to Achilles with his proposal to send *him* to battle instead; it was again associated with a sudden decision to go forward. This formulaic gestural mannerism of a physical act directed against the bodily self dramatically underlines the resolve to act, overcoming a conflict and accepting something heretofore unacceptable – a crucial moment in the psychological development of character. The character's forward action is against great resistance, against the wish to stop the progression of time. The consequences are predictable and, on a deeper level, known to Achilles already. He strikes both his thighs, as Patroklos had done earlier: The (double) body will be smitten and fall. Going along with time signifies the demise of the body.

Things now move quickly. Patroklos falls, slain by Apollo and Hektor. Numerous apostrophes here highlight the irrevocable advance of time by pointedly stressing that the future is already past. In XVI: 795 Achilles' crested helmet (worn by Patroklos) is thrown for the first time to the ground, smeared in blood and dust: Achilles is, symbolically, already dead! His immortal horses (given to Patroklos for the battle), now immobile like a funeral monument, are weeping for the fallen Patroklos. Zeus, seeing the horses, is touched with pity: "Ah unhappy pair ... Of all things that breathe and move on earth there is nothing more sorrowful than man" (XVII: 443-7). Grief and *mourning* – to be noted, first shown by the immortals (Achilles' mother Thetis, Zeus, and the immortal horses) – will be, from now on, the dominant mood. The human concern that Achilles showed in XI: 611 entails a heavy price. Psychic pain, genuine sadness, until now omnipotently excluded, will be felt in their full force.

When Antilochos arrives with the news of Patroklos' death, he finds Achilles "boding in his heart what had already taken place." The future is already past, and now, for the first time, Achilles realizes that his own mortality is actual. The death of his "double" brings him face-to-face with his own dead self. The use of Patroklos, dressed up as Achilles, riding Achilles' chariot (to everyone's eyes, the very image of Achilles himself) and then being struck down, was Homer's masterly invention that allowed him both to suggest the scene of the hero's own eventual death as well as unveil the whole range of Achilles' complex reactions in facing death. Patroklos' death is the only instance in the *Iliad* in which a god (Apollo), with his own hand, vanquishes a hero. Hektor will then finish him off. This is an echo of Achilles' own death by Apollo and by another of Priam's sons (Paris) which is to take place soon, as is recounted in the post-Homeric *Aethiopis*. We are thus presented here with a shadow play of Achilles' death through the use of allusion, which makes it all the more poignant. The scene here of Achilles, rolling in dust "outstretched mightily in his might" (XVIII: 26) upon hearing the news of Patroklos' death, is a scene of Achilles' death. This same formula ("outstretched mightily in his might") appears in the *Odyssey* (24: 40) describing, there, the actual death of

Achilles himself. And, as in the *Odyssey* scene, here too Achilles' mother Thetis and her sisters, the water-nymphs Nereids, rush up to his side from their dwelling place in the depths of the Ocean. Thetis here in the *Iliad* is mourning her son (who is lamenting the loss of his friend) as if it were *he* who is dead: "I shall never again welcome him returning home," she says wailing and holding up Achilles' head in her hands, a ritualistic funeral gesture (XVIII: 71).

For Aristotle (*Poetics* 1452b 9-10), a tragic plot comprises three elements: *peripeteia* (Reversal of the Situation), *anagnorisis* (Recognition, i.e., a new knowledge), and *pathos* (Suffering). All three are present here, giving the *Iliad* an un-mistakenly tragic cast. Patroklos' death brings about an unexpected reversal of the situation as a result of which Achilles comes to recognize who he really is, that is to know for the first time in an *immediate* sense his limits and his mortality, this leading, in turn, to his personal transformation in the course of his encounter with Priam. And there is suffering. A profound change in his self-image inaugurates Achilles' *metabasis*. In XVIII: 107, as we have seen, he bemoans "Oh, would that Strife and Anger perish ..." His thoughts from now on turn more frequently to his own death and the references to it become more prominent, frequent and explicit (XVIII: 95, 101, 329; XIX: 409, 420; XXI: 110; XXII: 360; XXIII: 126, 150, 244; XXIV: 131, 540). In a most touching scene in XXI: 106-113, his words to Priam's son, Lykaon, who is pleading with him to spare his life, express in a way that we have not heard before all the pain and compassion that stem from his now deeply felt awareness of the inevitability of death:

> *But, friend, you, too, die now; why such lament?*
> *Patroklos too, a man much superior to you, also died.*
> *And do you not see how I, too, am handsome and mighty?*
> *The son of a noble father, and a goddess was the mother that bore me.*
> *Yet over me, too, hang death and powerful fate.*
> *There shall come a dawn or an evening or a mid-day*
> *when my life too will be taken in battle by someone,*
> *striking me with a spear or an arrow sprung from a string.*

Time will not be stopped. Once again Achilles repeats "We will let things go on their way, even though we suffer" (XVIII: 112) and takes the crucial decision to go forward and return to battle himself.

However, the newly-achieved recognition of time and mortality, of one's vulnerability, brings about a violent reaction of uncontrollable sadistic rage and hatred. Achilles' fighting is of unimaginable cruelty. He is ruthless, full of disdain for his opponents, untouched by their suffering, pitiless. These are apocalyptic scenes of flood and conflagration. The River, in anguish, "choked with corpses," angrily protests that he cannot pour his lovely streams into the bright sea (XXI: 218-20). It seems that the realization of limits and the pain of loss cannot be easily tolerated in the psyche and mobilize powerful retrogressive forces of fierce persecutory rage and renewed omnipotence, which is what we see here in Achilles. Soon, he comes face-to-face with Hektor. Remember that Hektor's "body is covered by the armor that he had stripped from Patroklos" (XXII: 323). Achilles drives his spear through Hektor's collar bones and, thus, Achilles' *second* "double" falls in the dust in an act of suicidal allusions (Devereux, 1978). The symbolic death of Achilles himself here becomes explicit through Thetis' recent words to him: "Straight away after Hektor's is your own death ready" (XVIII: 96). Achilles knows that Hektor's death means his own.

> *As the generation of leaves so is the generation of men,*
> *scattered on the earth by the wind ...*
> *One generation springs up, the other passes away* (VI: 146-9).

Lamenting Patroklos' loss after the slaying of Hektor, Achilles falls asleep "on the shore of the deep-resounding sea." Patroklos' image appears to him, exactly as he looked in life, but as Achilles tries to embrace him, he clasps nothing, Patroklos' shadow vanishes like vapor, with the faint sound of a bird-cry. Achilles, bewildered ($ταφων$), leaps up and slaps his hands together (XXIII: 101-2). This gesture recalls the slapping of thighs earlier, which we linked to a resolve to go forward, to let time advance, symbolizing an assault on the body. Here we see the final result, the unavoidable consequence of that movement of time: At the end there is absence, no-thing. We might say that what Achilles is struggling to integrate in the gesture of slapping his hands is the experience of an object which, at a certain moment, becomes thin air, absent: an absent object. It is at moments like this, as when a dead person is seen in a dream, Rohde (1893) argued in the nineteenth century, that the concept of *psyche* as an agency independent of the body made its first appearance in Western thought. But, in our terms, this is the moment that inaugurates a process as a result of which the loss of the object will become tolerable only through its mentalization and the formation of symbols. A concept of absence appears here which gives substance both to the absent object and, also, to the absent subject, to nothingness; in other words, it gives rise to the concept of death. It is now that we can say that Achilles' death has a personal, and an *im*-mediate meaning to him, and that he has come to know himself as a being of and in time.

Paradoxically and significantly the time experience that has resulted in the personal consciousness of death is not an element of that consciousness itself: Death is timeless. Death *is*, it is *now*, an actuality, not an event of a future time. Put differently, the future is now; in the experience of death, all time is condensed in the present: "Now, therefore, since I *am not* returning to my beloved native land ..." says Achilles (XXIII: 150). This timeless present of death is expressed in the act of the *two hands coming together* in a vain attempt to collapse the void and to establish a continuity, to bridge an un-bridgeable gap between presence and absence, between the time of dream and the time of wakefulness, the time of wish and that of reality, the time of the present's future (the object will not be/is not there) and the time of the future's past (the object was/is there). And, as these two times collide on awakening (cf. the striking of the hands together), they produce a bewilderment in the "I" and an urgent attempt to eliminate the experienced discontinuity. This initiates the process of symbol-formation that will bridge the chasm. There is a noteworthy semantic ambiguity in Greek: The noun ταφος used in the scene of Achilles' dream to express "bewilderment" also means "burial of the dead": the bewilderment of absence.

What will follow now is the last Book with the striking scene of reconciliation that we discussed above, representing the culmination of the profound changes in Achilles. As already mentioned, the dominant theme after Book XVIII, and especially in the last two Books, is mourning, which goes on both in the Greek camp and in Troy.

The Song ends with *taphoi*. Jacqueline de Romilly (1991) of the Académie Française will point out: "No epic in the whole world has ever had a less triumphant conclusion."

The above reading, centered on the hero's relation to time, is admittedly one of many possible readings of the *Iliad*. It is a reading that wishes to be close to a listening, which of course was the original medium of the epic – a reading with eyes closed as it were, as could be the eyes of the listener, and as tradition wants the eyes of the Bard. Poetry's shut eyes point to its intimate relation to the dream.

The *Iliad* and the character of Achilles is above all analysis, Whitman (1958) reminds us. To analyze Achilles is not our intention here. To learn from Homer, yes. In any event, Homer was not interested in the psychology of an individual, but in universal principles that shape and express human reality. In that, he was closer to philosophy, which, at any rate, is the nature of poetry, as Aristotle tells us (*Poetics* 1451b 5-7). Homer, according to Whitman (1958), was the first to imagine a "figure who would typify, not material triumph, but the triumph of the spirit amid self-destruction," and was the first to dramatize "this paradox as the search for the integrity of the self against a panoramic background involving all the forces of the world, human and divine" (p. 220).

EPILEGOMENA

> *Be, and yet know the Non-Being's condition, the endless foundation of your inmost vibration, so that, this once, you may give it your perfect assent.*
> R. M. Rilke, *Sonnets to Orpheus* 2:13.

We suggested that the hero, at the beginning of the narration, is "blinded" by *Ate* and, ever so conscious of his divine origins, is profoundly sensitive to injuries to his esteem and unable to accept compromises. His knowledge of his mortality, early on, lacks depth, it is only "what he has been told" it is external knowledge, we might say. It could be argued that his relations (to Briseis, or to

Patroklos) do not seem to be relations to separate objects, independent of the self, but rather to parts of himself, to "subjective objects" (Winnicott, 1971, p. 71). MacCary (1982) sees prominent narcissistic elements in Homer's Achilles' character.[14] He claims that Achilles' objects are, in fact, selfobjects, and that he is incapable of desiring an object since he can only desire himself.

When challenged, Achilles flies into a narcissistic rage – the μῆνις which is characteristic of him – and is filled with intense persecutory hatred. But then comes the turning point that was mentioned above which sets the course of action in an entirely different direction. The concern shown in XI as he re-emerges from his omnipotent isolation (even though his concern is rather disguised behind motives of self-interest) plunges him *volens nolens* into the orbit of time, and what this brings on is the realization of limits, loss, and the pains of sadness. A transient regressive flight into omnipotent ruthlessness following Patroklos' loss passes away and leaves Achilles behind as a transformed man. It is not that there had not been earlier signs of the humane side of this most complex character. When he overpowers Iphition, for instance, his words to the fallen warrior, far from being exultant, sound more like a lament: "Here you lie, son of Otrynteus, most glorious of all men. Here is your death, though your birth was by Lake Gyge, where the lands of your fathers are, near Hyllos teeming with fish, and eddying Hermos." This is indeed an epitaph, a monument erected by Achilles himself to his victim. What happens in Book XXIV, however, is that, as a result of certain specific developments, Achilles' humane side becomes much more prominent. We believe that these developments have to do with his full integration of time and mortality.

Ever since Heidegger's monumental opus *Being and Time* appeared in 1926, it is not possible to examine the "I"'s relation to Time without reference to him. This is a remarkable work of, at times, impenetrable density and obscurity by a philosopher who is considered by some as one of the greatest thinkers of the twentieth century. Human existence, the "I" or personal consciousness (what Heidegger calls *Dasein*) is temporal, fundamentally "ek-static", that is, defined by Time along its three "ekstases" of future, past, and present. Achilles is "static", keeping himself outside the flow of events, until the crucial turning point of the first signs of *Sorge* (Care). It is only after his recognition and acceptance of the immanence of death that he will become what Heidegger calls a "whole" *Dasein*. A whole *Dasein* is a self that has integrated into its being the potentiality of non-being, of death, of absence. This is expressed by the attitude – we might call it "position" in the Kleinian sense – of "Being-towards-death" (*Sein zum Tode*). It involves a leap forward, the *Dasein* "getting ahead of itself", "running forward" (*Vorlaufen*), an act that renders the

---

[14] My misgivings about MacCary's thesis is that if Achilles represents in fact a "narcissistic personality disorder" as defined by Kohut, or a "borderline" à la Kernberg and nothing more, as MacCary argues, and if there is no movement, no evolution to something else, we would be hard put to explain the extent of the *Iliad*'s diachronic appeal.

potentiality of death actual and certain. Achilles' gesture of slapping the thighs and his expression "Let things move on" clearly dramatize this state of mind. Schadewaldt (1965) astutely observes that the principle that governs Homer's world is the "principle of the presence of the future" (p. 398), "living the future in the present" (p. 65).

The centrality of death, the nucleus of authentic wholeness in Heidegger's sense, leads Griffin (1980) to characterize the *Iliad* as a poem of death, of the constant transition between life and death. "It is part of the greatness of Achilles" Griffin says "that he is able to contemplate and accept his own death more fully and more passionately than any other hero" (p. 95); he is tragic because he knows that he is victor and victim at once (p. 55).

According to Heidegger, the whole *Dasein* experiences death as a personal fact, immanent to the "I": Only then is the "Being-towards-death" authentic. Authenticity is achieved by a *Dasein* that frees itself from the (blind) comfort of its absorption in and dependence on the values and pursuits of an impersonal collectivity, the "They", or "One does" (*Man*). In psychoanalytic terms, a submission of this type corresponds to the Winnicottian "false self" (Winnicott, 1965). Achilles frees himself from the constraints of the "They" heroic code (honor, physical prowess) that had guided his actions until now only in the final scene with Priam, by committing an act which was *not* part of that code (precisely the reason which prompts Kirk to find it "unnerving").

The authentic whole self will act, from now on, no longer because it is so ordained by Moira but by assuming personal responsibility. Moira will, ultimately, be recognized as a projection outwards of the responsibility for actions whose origin is, in fact, internal. Moira is a form of the Heideggerian "They." Admittedly the notion of an independently acting human agency, of personal Will, does not exist in Homeric times but what we see in the *Iliad* (i.e., at the infancy of Western civilization), are the labor pains of its birth. It corresponds to a certain stage of the development of the infant when the dominance of projective identification diminishes, as projected ego parts are recovered and relocated within the self.

The supreme human task, it seems, is to articulate Necessity, a force imposed from without, with human Will. The Homeric hero struggles to coalesce the Ought and the Will into one. This is the meaning of Heidegger's notion of "getting ahead," towards death. The hero actively *pursues* his pre-determined fate with resoluteness (*Entschlossenheit*). He strives to *will* his mortal destiny, even though it lies fundamentally outside the domain of his power, and to attain human freedom. This freedom however is by its very nature tragic. It is tragic because it is predicated on the condition of willing what cannot be willed (since there is no possibility of not willing). This is the foundational existential paradox that establishes tragic free Will.

The "whole *Dasein*" in time comes to know that it is the "I" which is the creator of much that humans ascribe to Moira. The whole (temporal) self can then, through its actions, break the chain of Ananké and be causal in a personal sense, thus shaping its own mortal destiny rather than being at the mercy of Fate.

In Book XXIV, Achilles' authentic whole *Dasein* emerges in the progression from θαμβεειν to θαυμαζειν. When Priam arrives at Achilles' camp, the latter's reaction is awe. Priam, at this point, is a persecutory object to Achilles (Achilles knows that Priam's son, Paris, will soon slay him). Priam, for his part, comes to Achilles' camp as if he were going to the House of the Dead to retrieve Hektor, and Achilles, after all, has brought on the death of his family, of his whole kingdom. When the two men look at each other they contemplate death and experience awe, the Heideggerian Angst. One-hundred-and-fifty lines later, however, awe has changed to marvel. Persecutory anxiety has given its place to a depressive attitude towards the object. The hated/hating object (Priam) and the loving/loved object (Peleus) have become one for Achilles. Good and bad are no longer split,[15] splitting having given way to ambivalence (cf. XXIV: 569). Thus, in the end, Achilles' full acceptance of the reality of time, allowing him to accept the image of a limited, mortal self ("whole" *Dasein*), enables him to allow for the co-existence of good and bad in what Melanie Klein calls a "whole" object, and to be ruthful.[16]

A remarkable feature of the moment of *thaumazein* is the *terpos* (the joy felt in gazing at each other)[17], which recalls Freud's "*joyful 'da'*", in his grandson's *Fort-Da* game (Freud, 1920, p. 14). The full significance of that game for the child becomes clear in Freud's footnote: "It soon turned out, however, that during this long period of solitude (the absence of the boy's mother) he had found a method of making *himself* disappear. He had discovered his reflection in a full-length mirror which did not quite reach to the ground, so that by crouching down he could make his mirror-image 'gone.'" Thus, the re-finding of the absent object is tied to the re-finding of the absent self, and this is a pivotal moment in the development and consolidation of an integrated ego. The absent object, in the Kleinian schema, is the destroyed and hence persecutory object. But now, as the two men gaze at each other at the end of the Book XXIV scene (i.e., after their reconciliation), they contemplate a *repaired object*, a *repaired self*. The joy that comes from re-finding the object in Freud's sense is the joy associated with the reparation of the object and the corresponding reparation of the self.[18]

---

[15] Note, by the way, the harmonious co-existence of good and evil in the Shield of Achilles' new armor, brought to him by his mother, in XVIII: 478-608: The totality of life's tragic contradictions are depicted here side by side.

[16] It might be suggested that the articulation of present and absent selfobject that gives rise to the symbolic object and the concept of the mortal self opens the way for the coming together of the good and the bad object in the formation of the Kleinian whole object.

[17] See p. 12: ταρπησαν (they enjoyed).

[18] One could speculate that the joy or pleasure associated with epic poetry (see, e.g., the *terpos* of Achilles singing in IX: 186), is related to its reparative function. Homer seems to point to the reparative effect of poetry when he has Helen say, in VI: 357-8, that

Acceptance of responsibility for the destructiveness inherent in instinctual life, giving rise to concern, guilt and reparative attempts, is a major achievement in human development, as the Kleinians have underlined. It comes after the use of omnipotence as a defense against depression is diminished, and after "the sanctification of grievance and revenge" recede, as Brenman (1985) aptly points out. Such changes become possible when depressive affect is better tolerated owing to the self's toleration and integration of the absence of the object and the toleration of separateness. The process involves mourning, which, for Achilles, meant mourning for the loss of his omnipotence and acceptance of his own mortality. What Achilles had to mourn was ultimately the loss of an idealized internal selfobject – an immortal mother – from whom he had to eventually separate. Genuine empathy, as we see it in the Book XXIV scene, is then possible – empathy with a separate object which is recognized as being other and different, yet *similar* to the self (identification now replacing projective identification).

The capacity to recognize the similar in what is different is the basis of *metaphora*, in Aristotle's view (*Poetics* 1459a 8). The object that Achilles and Priam are gazing at in this scene is a metaphorized object: The end of Achilles' *metabasis*, we might say, is to arrive at the position of *metaphora*. A process of mourning for the lost object has taken place that has led further to the emergence of symbolic thought, and symbols are reparative (of absence). Thus Achilles caringly lifts Hektor's anointed body onto the bier.

Heidegger's Guilt (*Schuld*), which is essentially a "negative" concept referring to a "deficit" or "debt" for having fallen into the in-authenticity of taking cover in anonymity ("They") and for having been passively "thrown" into this world, gives rise to a sense of personal responsibility and to Care (*Sorge*) for the *Dasein*'s objects. It is care that directs the *Dasein* towards future projects. The psychoanalytic and, more specifically, Kleinian notion of guilt, viewed from a different perspective (active), also leads to attempts at reparation and to caring for the object once its absence has been tolerated and integrated into the self. Psychoanalytic thinking, here, converges with philosophical speculation, even though by following different routes.

The role of *Litae* (goddesses personifying repentance and forgiveness) in "remedying" (IX: 507) the damage wrought by *Ate* should be noted in this context. Such an action facilitates emotional *katharsis* through the process of reparation. It is clear that a movement from wrath to ruth reflects an underlying ethical design in the *Iliad* (Jaeger, 1973, p. 48), and this was not missed even by Homer's first commentator in Antiquity, Theagenes of Rhegium (sixth century BCE).

The compassion and concern of the last scene take us back to where we started, that is, to the turning point of XI when Achilles first shows the sign

---

the evil doom sent by Zeus is to "become a song for men that are yet to be." See Chapter Two.

of concern that initiated this whole movement. A self-sustaining cycle is completed (consisting of concern, leading to the acknowledgement of time, which leads to caring). Before concluding we shall have to say a few things about that cycle.

The movement that involves the integration of time, loss and mourning, reparation, care and concern for injuries inflicted is set into motion by mother. The role of Thetis is crucial to these developments in the *Iliad*. Thetis appears at three pivotal points in the narrative: at the beginning, in the middle and at the end, or in Books I, XVIII-XIX and XXIV, respectively. Her function is composite and consistent in all three: she introduces time, limits, loss and mourning, compassion and reparation. In her first lines she mourns her son whose life is to be short and sorrowful: "Oh my son, why did I rear you, having borne you to dreadful calamities!" (I: 414). In her last lines she encourages him to bring an end to his paralyzing grief, to take food, to take pleasure in love making, and to release Hektor's body, reconciling himself with the dead (XXIV: 128-137).

What mother introduces and what the infant introjects is the capacity to tolerate absence and to deal with aggression. It is *her* capacity to integrate time that the infant first introjects (Winnicott, 1965)[19], and this capacity is based on her own success in having developed mechanisms for dealing with aggression and loss, such as reparation and symbolization. But once this is introduced from the outside, a cycle (Winnicott, 1958) may be started inside the infant, constituted of the two poles of destruction and repair. We suggest that what happens next is that, although time was first an introjection from the outside, the subsequent movement inaugurated inside, involving an *alternation between destruction and reparation*, generates time *internally*, now as a *lived* experience. This leads to the authentication and consolidation of the "I"'s sense of time and completes the circle that started with introjection.

A distinction is thus made in this schema between what could be called "external" time (which could remain unassimilated, as e.g., in cases of "false self") and "internal" or authentically psychic time. In the end, a full integration of time signifies that a "whole" object (Klein) and a "whole" subject (Heidegger) have been achieved. This gives rise to the capacity for compassion and caring for the object altered by time (damaged, absent) and to reparative acts, which, in turn, further consolidate time by establishing a mechanism for its internal generation.

If we look at this process in greater detail we could speculatively locate the earliest point in human development at which a rudimentary inner sense of time may first appear. Adequate maternal function (which, according to Winnicott, includes among other things "holding time" for the time being) leads

---

[19] Winnicott (1965) tells us that "time is kept going by the mother and this is one aspect of her auxiliary ego-functioning", and that the infant comes to have a personal time-sense only as long as he can keep alive the imago of the mother in the inner world (p. 77).

to the infant's increased capacity to tolerate destructive impulses, and this leads to a diminution of projective identification, with the result that a more firm boundary is formed around the developing "I," which, therefore, becomes fleetingly, a separate unit with limits and limitations. We can now speak of the beginning of an "inside" and an "outside." It may be precisely at this point where there is a rapid and irregular *oscillation between fusion with mother and separateness* that there first appears an inchoate sense of time as the product of such repeated and alternating radical alterations in the state of being (See Chapter Three). With the increasing solidification of the infant's "I-ness" and the recognition of the effects of its own destructiveness on its internal objects, the cycle of attack—repair referred to above enters into play, significantly reinforcing the sense of time and giving rise to a sense of duration.

It will be noted that this view of the generation of the sense of time is different from Freud's (1925) theory (Freud calls it only a "suspicion"), according to which the ego's sense of time derives from the discontinuity of the periodic cathexis of the perceptual system (Pcpt-Cs) and its withdrawal.[20] That leans more towards a cognitive model, whereas the view proposed here emphasizes affective movements in relation to the object as being at the origin. From another perspective, Hartocollis (1983), in his comprehensive examination of the concept of time, believes that "one may speak of time – and I speak here about psychological, lived, or subjective time – as a dimension of affectivity ..." (p. 77). Arlow (1986), on the other hand, locates the roots of the sense of time in the physiological interval between instinctual need and satisfaction. It could be suggested, however, that the capacity of the infant to remain integrated and in a state of anticipation during this interval depends in some capacity on keeping alive and intact a "good," nourishing internal object. It is the insertion of the *object* in the gap between need and satisfaction that creates a continuity in a series of discontinuities and is responsible for the sense of time, for self-identity across time and for object constancy. However, unless the (introjected) object is subsequently integrated through an internal process which involves the *linking* of the absent/damaged object with the need-satisfying/repaired object there can be no lasting consolidation of the sense of time and no thoroughgoing sense of a temporal self.

The rhythm of a continuous alternation between destructive attack on the object and restitution or repair promotes the construction of a bridge, as it were, over the gulf between the two, and this becomes the foundation of hope. Hope, giving substance to the interval and affirming continuity, provides the

---

[20] It should be specified that Freud's *theory of time* is a complex one involving as it does the axis of need-satisfaction/frustration, postponement of action, anticipation of fulfillment, repetition, as well as primary-secondary functioning, all this being further complicated by the superimposition of the mechanism of *Nachträglichkeit*. Freud did not explicitly work out the details of a complete theory of time but his thoughts on the *origin* of our sense of time are stated in the *Mystic Pad* and had also appeared earlier in *Beyond the Pleasure Principle*, S.E. 18: 28.

infrastructure for the defining characteristic of the evolved sense of time, namely, its *spiral* nature,[21] which in turn is the condition that makes reparation possible. Linear time constrains the ego in agonizing compulsive back-and-forth movements which obstruct genuine creative change.

It thus becomes clear that primitive aggression and constructive acts are in-dissociable from each other and are indispensable for the above developments and for the capacity to change. It is aggression that leads to creative restitution, and it is the possibility of making restitution that frees the ego from excessive constricting inhibitions. Nietzsche's (2006) Zarathustra asserts "Only where there are graves can there also be resurrection" (p. 85).

A word may be added, before concluding, about reparation and creativity. It could be argued that in the Achilles—Priam encounter in Book XXIV something *new* is created and, since this novel event or state is the outcome of processes predominantly governed by the Life instinct, that scene can be seen as depicting the quintessential dynamic of the artistic creative impulse in the service of Eros. Kleinian thought has linked creativity with reparation, attributing to the latter a key role in aesthetics. However it would seem that, unless we postulate a creative drive that goes beyond the reparation of the object damaged in phantasy to encompass the impulse to fill in the vacant space of an object which is absent *independently* of the "I"'s actions, we cannot have an adequate account of genuine art or of creative scientific endeavor. The object in these circumstances is, of course, granted separateness and autonomy from the self, this being possible only after the infant's omnipotence has been optimally curtailed. However, the object's absence is not felt to be due to the self's attacks. A vacuum, a void, is acknowledged as independent of the self and beyond its control. The object that will be constituted to occupy this space of nothingness is the object of true art and of scientific discovery. Heidegger's concept of a whole *Dasein* is defined by the capacity to tolerate the dread of non-existence and to resolutely pursue projects that realize the *Dasein*'s potentialities. We would say that, in his sense, only the whole *Dasein* can be truly creative. Artistic activity, in going beyond, or rather before, the "damage-repair" cycle, creates its own (primal) time which revolves on the "presence-absence" axis. The crucial question of how and with what material the ego fills in the gap of the autonomously absent object cannot be dealt with here. The creation is clearly not *ex nihilo* and, as before, the presence of an alive nourishing good internal object is decisive to the process.

And so, after more than two-and-a-half millennia since the composition of the Epics, could one still say that Homer is a "teacher of humanity"? The answer would appear to be in the affirmative. Homer shows us that there is a link between an individual's full acceptance of time and mortality and his or her capacity for compassion that leads to acts of reparation aimed at injuries inflicted as an unavoidable consequence of being human. This explains Homer's diachronic actuality.

---

[21] Recurrence is on the basis of similarity, not of identity.

Chapter Two

Homer's theory of poetry
Psychoanalytic notes on the primal metaphor

The stranger has arrived at Alkinoos' court, in Scheria, the island of the Phaeakians (*Odyssey*, 8). He came from the sea, washed off in a lonely beach, found by the young princess. "Listen to me, leaders and counselors," now proclaims the king, "so that I may tell you what is in my heart. This stranger, I know not who he is, has come to my house in his wanderings but is now eager to move on ..." The urgency in the stranger's forward movement, however, must be coupled with a turn to the past. The blind bard Demodokos, bearer of memory, is summoned. He is the voice of the Muse, daughter of the goddess *Mnemosyne*, who has been an eyewitness to all that has taken place. So Demodokos has seen it all, being himself present, as it were, when the events that he is now called upon to recount occurred. It is as if he is presently the only one who can set forward the course of the black ship that will carry the stranger to his final destination. And so he begins his "sweet song" of the glorious deeds of men, taken from "the lay whose fame had reached wide heaven," the lay of the Great War. Instead of *terpos* (delight), however, the song brings tears to the stranger's eyes.

> *Why do you weep stranger, asks the king, why do you wail in your heart as you hear the fate of the Argives and of Troy? This the gods brought about, and spun the thread of ruin for men, so that there may be song for those yet to come. (Odyssey 8: 577-580)*

Taken at face value this is a puzzling statement. All that suffering for the sake of a song for future generations! We find the same idea again in the *Iliad*. Here, it is spoken by Helen:

> *Zeus has brought an evil doom on us, that even in days to come we may be a song for men that are yet to be. (Iliad, VI: 357-8).*

This theme, repeated as it is, posits a direct link between human suffering and poetry (*aoidé*). The link appears to be causal (ινα, ως): Suffering leads to poetry, or is the reason for poetry, its source. What is implied is that suffering calls for poetry, transforms itself into poetry, consumes itself in poetry, even finds its justification in poetry. Since "delight" is the natural effect of poetry (8: 45, 8: 429, 17: 385), suffering can be said to, in some mysterious manner, undo itself in poetry. What is, therefore, indirectly suggested here, for the first time, is a sort of *therapeutic* effect of poetry, poetry being a counterweight or an antidote for human suffering. Four centuries later, Aristotle, in his *Poetics*, will elaborate his "cathartic" theory of tragic poetry, echoing a traditional view of poetry's healing capacity, a view that can be traced, as we see here, to the early days of oral composition.

It would seem, then, that the task of poetry, according to Homer, is to tell of human *pathos* and to bring about a transformation and a relief of suffering. In so doing it brings humans into a relation with each other across time. The transfer of disastrous destiny to *epos* (word), affirmed in the two excerpts we saw, is, thus, expressly associated with a) the transfer or passage to others and b) the passage of time.

METAPHORA

Like Molière's M. Jourdain (*Le bourgeois gentilhomme*, Act II, Scene 4), humanity must have been speaking poetically long before it had any awareness of doing so, and ever since it came to know suffering. Heidegger (1949) held that poetry is the founding of Being through words and, as such, it is "the primal language of an historical people." What we suggest here is that the poetic act is a liminal act situated at the origins of humanization, at the point of the emergence of language, of a sense of time and of the consciousness of the self. It must have appeared at the earliest evolutionary moment of the "transfer," or transition, from a purely biological level of existence to a mental/psychic level. Metaphor (*meta-pherein* = to trans-port, to trans-fer) is, not surprisingly, the quintessence of poetry since poetry was born at the moment of that transition (see e.g., Brooks, 1947; Lakoff & Turner, 1989; Tate, 1942). It was Aristotle who first stated emphatically that to have command of metaphor is the greatest thing in poetry (*Poetics* 1459a 6). The *mimesis* of tragedy is essentially the transfer of an action onto the level of *mythos* (= speech, poetic tale); it is the metaphorization of an action. The most elemental form of the process of metaphorization is the alphabet, considered by Novalis as well as Mallarmé to be the greatest work of poetry (Jakobson, 1987, p. 370). Representing, as it does, the transposition of basic bodily sounds onto a system of abstract signs, the alphabet is pure metaphor.

Poetry, then, although difficult, if not impossible, to define, has been considered to be the art of metaphor. *Poiein* is *metapherein*. The accumulated literature on metaphor over the centuries, comprising studies by literary theorists, philologists, linguists, philosophers, cognitive psychologists as well as psychoanalysts, is indeed impressive, both in its volume and diversity. No attempt will be made here to review this vast field, but, before looking at some contemporary work in this area, we must revisit Aristotle's influential definition of metaphor.

"Metaphor," Aristotle tells us, "is the application (*epipherein*) of an alien name" (*Poetics* 1457b 8). This definition underscores the fundamental non-isomorphism between the two elements linked by the metaphoric process:

The name applied to the particular situation is imported from elsewhere and is alien. Now, since according to Aristotle the conjunction of things which are not naturally attached to each other constitutes an *aenigma* (*Poetics* 1458a 27), metaphors are, by their very nature, enigmatic (*Rhetoric* 1405b 6). To be the master of metaphor is by far the greatest thing for the poet, he says, but, in his view, it cannot be taught. It is a sign of genius, for it consists in the capacity to discern the similar in the different (*Poetics* 1459a 6-8). The poetic act is, therefore, bringing together in what appears to be a paradoxical fashion what is seemingly discrepant and unrelated; it is bringing disparate elements into relation with each other, thereby establishing heretofore unknown links.

Linguists and philosophers, studying metaphor as a figure of speech, as a particular way we use language, have shown that all metaphors are rooted in the body, called the "source domain," and consist of the relocation of this concrete field of experience in the non-physical, abstract realm of the mind, called the "target domain" (Lakoff & Johnson, 1980; Lakoff & Turner, 1989). It is held that "the essence of all metaphor is understanding and experiencing one kind of thing in terms of another" (Lakoff & Johnson, 1980, p. 5). There is, accordingly, an epistemic value in metaphorization in that it allows for the understanding of something more elusive in terms of what is more immediate and given to the senses. It is the attempt to understand the unfamiliar by the familiar.

Johnson (1987) invokes the notion of "image schemata," which are structures emerging "at the level of our bodily movements through space, our manipulation of objects, and our perceptual interactions" and which we use to organize our comprehension of anything meaningfully (mental level) (p. 29). Such schemata are: container (inside—outside), surface, contact, object, merging, splitting, full-empty, blockage, verticality (up-down), and so forth. Their direct relevance to psychoanalytic models of early development describing the relation between mother and infant is obvious.

The particular significance of such studies is that they have gradually moved away from the narrow view of metaphor as a figure of speech – one of the *tropes* of Ancient rhetoric – and have come to regard it as the fundamental mode of mental functioning and of all knowledge possible to humans. That all thought and language is inherently metaphorical had already been pointed out by Nietzsche (1976) with his usual precocious insightfulness, and, in this century, by Cassirer (1946), by Arendt (1977), by Gadamer (1975), and others. Cassirer (1946, p. 85ff) places metaphor at the root of language where it is embedded, on a pre-symbolic level, in a "concentration and heightening of simple sensory experience."

What follows from all this is the conclusion that we come to understand the world – inner and outer – and to construct and ascribe meaning to it, in terms of our basic bodily experiences. The image we form of reality is the product of projecting, as it were, our body outwards or inwards. Concepts and the words that express them are cast in terms of experiences of the body. Richards (1936), after stressing that all thought is metaphoric (p. 94), reminds us that "historians of language have long taught that we can find no word or description for any of the intellectual operations which, if its history is known, is not seen to have been taken, by metaphor, from a description of some physical happening" (p. 91). Metaphor, therefore, as the omnipresent canon of thought and as "a pervasive principle of human understanding," (Johnson, 1987, p. 65) is shown by contemporary studies to have its origin in the body. The body is the "vehicle," to use Richard's terminology (Richards, 1936. p. 96), of our most abstract conceptualizations and of their expression in language. The very concept of "metaphor," itself, is a metaphor, deriving from the displacement of a physical body in space (*meta-pherein*). And so is "language" (*lingua* = tongue). Notably, the concept of *"psyche"*, as well, emerges from the bodily experience of breathing (*psychein* = to breathe).

The notion that the defining characteristic of humans and what differentiates them from animals is their capacity to move beyond bodily sense perception to conceptual constructions is very old. It was first enunciated by Alkmaion of Kroton, a physician-philosopher who lived in the sixth century BCE. Man's distinguishing characteristic, he held, is his capacity to *xynienai*, while animals remain on the level of sensation (Kirk, 1971, p. 233 Fr. 284). *Xynienai* means "to put together," to bring elements together, to relate them to each other, and this is equated, in Alkmaion's surviving fragment, with "thinking" (*phronein*), conceiving relations between disparate things. This finds its echo in Aristotle's "enigmatic conjunctions" that characterize metaphor, as if all thinking cannot be but metaphoric. We already have here, in Alkmaion, an allusion to the primordial kinship between thinking and metaphor and their emergence from the sensory body.

The emphasis that studies in the humanities place on the body as the origin of metaphor, thought, and language comes as no surprise to the psychoanalyst who is aware that "the ego is first and foremost a bodily ego" (Freud, 1923, p. 25). Ella Sharpe (1950) in her 1940 article on metaphor draws attention to "the physical basis and experience from which metaphoric speech springs" and suggests that there is a "subterranean passage between mind and body" underlying this process. She postulates that "metaphor can only evolve in language or in the arts when the bodily orifices become controlled" (p. 156). Unrelieved physical tension is discharged through speech, "so that we may say speech in itself is a metaphor [of released bodily contents], that metaphor is as ultimate as speech" (p. 157). B. Lewin (1971) argues that models of the mind themselves are metaphors originating in the body and the body image. He traces the process of evolution from the body to the idea of the body. Rogers (1978) asserts that the poet's own body is a rich mine of metaphorical ore, and points to the ubiquitous presence of body imagery in poetry which adds vitality to it as it stimulates the primary process of mentation associated with creativity (p. 78). "The needs of the body," Rogers (1978) states, "speak through the body of language which is the language of the body" (p. 85). Marion Milner (1957) had already shown the direct link between creative capacity and the various bodily functions. Melnick (1997) contends that the image schemata operant in the metaphoric process derive from activity in the erogenous zones of libidinal development, and that many character traits as well as symptoms are metaphorical expressions of early experiences connected with one or another bodily zone. "Truth is metaphoric and bodily and fuzzy," Holland (1999) concludes in a recent contribution.[22]

We must now return to the poet, that supreme craftsman of metaphor, and to the poetic act of "making" (*poiein*) something new through the transformation (*metaphora*) or transubstantiation of the body. Swaying endlessly on a tense tightrope drawn on one end by the body and on the other by something called "thought," the poet is a creature of the "in-between," of an area arching over a chasm. Between Nietzsche's (1954) dionysian and apollonian worlds, in that indefinable "intermediate area" of Winnicott's (1971), the poet is the instrument of Schiller's *Spieltrieb*. Schiller (1943) held that man is caught in the relentless antagonism of the two primordial drives of Senses (*sinnlicher Trieb*) and Form (*Formtrieb*) and strives to realize himself through the intervention of a conciliatory Play drive (*Spieltrieb*) which expresses itself in art. Only the activity of this drive can bring about the harmonization of the other two opposing drives and achieve a measure of aesthetic freedom, that is, freedom from the immediate demands of the senses (*aesthesis*).[23]

But the stakes in the poet's tightrope play are high. His "references" are radically "split" (Ricoeur, 1979) as he attempts to become the vehicle of an unbearable "modal ambiguity" (Rogers, 1978, p. 53) that seeks to establish links between two opposing poles of existence. Plato gave us a poignant metaphor of the poet's metaphoric project. We read in the *Ion* (534a 7 - 534b 2): "For the poets tell us, don't they, that they take their songs (*mele*) from rills that flow with honey in the gardens and glens of the Muses, and bring them as the bees bring honey (*meli*), flying in the same fashion." In Greek, the words "songs" and "honey" are nearly homophonous (*mele*, *meli*). The mystery lies in the leap from *meli* to *mele*, from the physical to the verbal. There is a paradoxical and enigmatic link here that defies categories and it is this link that defines the poetic act. The non-isomorphic character of the relation between the two elements brought together – what the scholastics called *inadaequatio* – is responsible for that indefinable something that defies the verbal register and constitutes the essence of poetry. It is as if the poetic is the elusive something after the word has been uttered, it is what is left behind, an inexpressible surplus of meaning; as if a poem is always already written in a foreign language and, as such, it is only partly translatable.

For the poet to be able to undertake the "flight" that precariously bridges the gulf between the body and the word, he must occupy a space of

---

[22] An epistemological caveat is in order at this point: the body in question, the body *in itself*, cannot be known except via its representations. Truth may be bodily but it is not *of* the body. We may know the somatic but not the soma itself. All discourse on the body is, of necessity, proximal to the speaker.

[23] Note that the notion of art as play is already present in Plato (*Politikos* 288c).

"madness," an area "outside rationality," according to Plato (*Ion* 534b 5-6). Here, in this Winnicottian transitional space of illusion, which is the soil of all creativity, a new reality is constructed which is paradoxical and enigmatic because it is the product of the combination of irreconcilable elements. Majorcan storytellers begin their tales with the exordium "*Aixo era y no era*" ("It was and it was not") (Jakobson, 1987, p. 86). The status of the new reality, the *poietic* thing, is fundamentally contradictory, inherently ambiguous, ontologically fuzzy and perpetually in transit, as it expresses the inherent dissonance of the human condition, to use Nietzsche's (1954) terminology (p. 1087). The (blind) poet's eye will discern "the before un-apprehended relations of things" and speak them in his "vitally metaphorical language," seeking forever fresh associations, Shelley (1965) tells us (VII, p. 111). Relations of things until now un-apprehended are "marked" by the poet, and a new reality emerges which is strangely familiar.

Now, if *metaphorein* is *poiein*, the "making" of something new consists of a process in which what appeared before as semantically incongruous acquires now a new semantic pertinence (Ricoeur, 1975, 1979) that allows it to become affectively congruous and personally meaningful. Ricoeur (1975) speaks of the metaphor's "semantic innovation," something analogous to scientific discovery, a "re-description of reality" (*Études* 6 and 7). Black's (1955, 1962, 1977) seminal studies on metaphor stress the "cognitive gain" that is yielded by the interaction between the metaphor's two referents. Rather than a mere substitution of A by B based on analogy (cf. Aristotle, *Poetics* 1457b 10 and *Rhet.* 1405a 11), Black proposes a semantic theory of transformative interaction that leads to the creation of new meaning. The innovation and the resulting gain, however, are not only semantic and cognitive, as these authors emphasize, but touch the psyche as a whole. The new meaning thus engendered will now act, *après coup*, on the originary referent, the body, modifying the way it is experienced. *Meli* (honey) leads to *mele* (songs), but as a result of *mele*, the experience of *meli* will never be the same.

The apicultural metaphor of the metaphoric process must not, however, obscure the fact that the status of *mele* is never stable, but is, as Plato suggested, "flighty" ("the poet is a light and flighty thing": *Ion,* 534b 3-4), in perpetual change, opening up to regions unknown. The *poietic* enterprise has no fixed goal or aim, which is what places it outside the realm of reason. There is a striking thought in Longinus (1990): We read in Homer, Longinus reminds us, that the gods' horses can leap as far as the eye can see (V:770-772); it would be understandable, therefore, says Longinus, if someone were to exclaim "But if the horses pushed forward with twice as much force, they would indeed be in *no place!*" This non-topos of imagination's leap beyond reason points to the fact that the poet's tightrope is held on one end by the body and on the other by *nothing*. The poetic act is, we might say, the body's dislocation into the Open, the non-topos which we call "phantasy", or "thought."

In the leap, the poetic function of language – what Jakobson (1987) calls "poeticity" – makes its appearance. The word here is no longer a mere representation of the thing, an indifferent reference to the physical reality from which it originated; rather, it has become itself a reality of its own (Jakobson, 1987, p. 378). But the persisting awareness of the fundamental inadequacy (the *inadaequatio*) of the correspondence between word and thing – that is, their non-isomorphism, which is the basis of poetic ambiguity (A is and is not B) – produces an unstable equilibrium which impels a mobility of signs and leads to an infinite chain of signification. Without this fluidity, Jakobson (1987) points out, the relationship between object and sign becomes automatized and metaphor dies. Metaphor is alive as long as *Aixo era y no era*.

It must be stressed, however, that to maintain the awareness of the *inadaequatio* the originary referent must not be lost sight of. And it *does* tend to be "forgotten" (repression). Man, it seems, is forever suspended between the forgotten and the unknown. It is here that poetic *Mnemosyne* fulfils its role. It is given license to resurrect the archaic body and to construct a poetic truth. But isn't *Mnemosyne* also the analyst's guiding principle as well?

Mnemosyne's daughter, the Muse, is the vehicle of history. She imparts her first-hand knowledge to the poet, who comes to experience in person and in the present the events that he recounts in his "divine song" (*Odyssey*, 8: 499). Poetic memory re-presents a historical reality (what the psychoanalyst calls psychic reality). In Heidegger (1962)'s terms, the poet's voice "discloses," "unconceals," or releases from forgetfulness the essence of Being and in so doing approaches truth (*a-lethia*). Heidegger reminds us that the Greek concept of *a-lethia* (truth) means "non-forgetfulness." The notion of recollection (*anamnesis*) of true events of the past, which are now buried and unavailable to immediate awareness but are potentially retrievable, had a long and influential history in Antiquity. It had its roots in Orphic religion, was passed on to the Pythagoreans, and was fully developed by Plato who held that all knowledge is recollection (*anamnesis*).

It must be quite obvious by now that there are intriguing analogies between the poetic-metaphoric process and the psychoanalytic process and we shall, later, turn our attention to these.

We will adopt, for the purposes of the present discussion, the term *primal metaphor* to designate the elemental process that involves the passage (*meta-phora*) from the bodily to the mental and the psychic. It is proposed that the primal metaphor is the process underlying both metaphor in the narrow sense, as a figure of speech, as well as metaphor in the broad, general sense of the metaphoric nature of all thought and language. If we regard thought as a metaphor of the body, and the poet's language as "flesh made word" (Rogers, 1978, p. 84), the primal metaphor is a reference to the body of thought.

IN THE COURT OF SCHERIA

Homer, as we have seen, believed that human sorrow and suffering is channeled into poetry. It is the basic stuff of poetry and its motive force. In the two relevant excerpts cited, Homer was probably expressing a traditional belief that he received as a formulaic theme from the rich stock of theme and motif formulae available to oral composers.

But why is this so? What happens when pain *is* transferred to words (*epea*) and narrated? In an attempt to answer this question we shall seek some "internal evidence" on the effects of this process, that is, from within the Epics themselves. We have an occasion of doing so by listening to the events of the Eighth Book of the *Odyssey* and what follows.

In Book 8, as we have seen, the bard Demodokos sings the tale of Odysseus' woes before the courtly audience and their guest, the stranger whose identity is still unknown. Demodokos' song is an *epos*-within-an-*epos*. The Muse, who "had been there in person," rouses him to sing of the Trojan campaign, of the violent strife which was "the beginning of all suffering" (8: 81). But, as we have seen, although the assembly of the Phaeakian nobles is taking pleasure in Demodokos' song, the stranger conceals his tears by covering his head with his purple cloak. The king notices this and proposes that the party switch to *physical* activities of entertainment instead (a "regression," we might say): jumping, boxing, running, dancing. When the lyre sings again, it is no longer about strife but about love, the love between Ares and Aphrodite, and the stranger takes great delight in this. He praises the minstrel above all mortal men for singing so well and truly of the suffering of the Achaeans, as if he himself were part of it. And then, strangely, he asks him to go back to the Trojan story and sing of the Wooden Horse which Odysseus cunningly led into the citadel, succeeding finally to penetrate into the sacred city. "If you tell me this tale rightly, I will straightaway declare to all mankind that the god has, in earnest, granted you the gift of divine song" (8: 496-498). The blind bard tells the glorious story of Odysseus and his comrades' entry into the "lofty City", their brave and terrible fight of destruction, their final victory. And, again, the stranger, listening intensely to the *aoidé*, "melts into tears" (8: 522):

> Like a woman wailing, throwing herself upon the body of her beloved husband who has fallen defending his city and his children, clinging tightly to him and shrieking aloud while she is being pulled away by enemy hands, her cheeks wasted with most pitiful grief, so was Odysseus shedding pitiful tears (8: 523-531)

A striking simile. As if, for a moment, these friendly Phaeakian hosts with their songs have become the enemy hands striving to tear Odysseus away from the beloved body. But whose body? Troy's? The maternal body that he strove to (re)enter and possess in that great campaign? His own body?

"Demodokos' resonant lyre does not give pleasure to all alike," remarks the king. To the noble assembly the minstrel's tales are *epea*, melodious words, but to the stranger these words are too close to his flesh and its pain. The time has now come. The king finally asks: "Who are you? Tell me the name by which your mother and father called you. No one (*outis*) is without a name" (8:

550-552). The stranger has been in his host's house for two days but is still nameless. And:

> *Tell me why you weep and wail deep in your heart listening to the misfortunes of the Argives and of Ilium. These the gods brought about and spun the skein of ruin for men so that there might be a song for those yet to be* (8: 577-580)

Only now, after his painful story has been narrated by Demodokos in the kind and welcoming atmosphere of Scheria's royal family, is the nameless stranger able to declare: "I am Odysseus, son of Laertes" (9: 19), thereby acquiring a name and an identity. And, now, he begins himself to recount his story and his sorrows, his own *epos* (the *Apologoi*). "Skillfully as a minstrel you tell your tale and your grievous woes," the king will exclaim to him later (11: 368-369). Over four Books (Books 9, 10, 11, 12) Odysseus narrates his misfortunes until his arrival at Scheria. An extended *epos*, sung this time by Odysseus himself, within Homer's "divine song."

It had not been noted, until relatively recently, that the sequence of scenes narrated by Odysseus in the *Apologoi* follows a pattern of ring composition which is familiar from elsewhere in the Homeric Epics (see Most, 1989, v. III, pp. 489-491). At the center of this narrative structure, at midpoint, lies the *Nekyia*, the descent of Odysseus to the world of the Dead, his *other journey* (10: 490). On either side of this (i.e., before and after the *Nekyia*) we have a set of events each set arranged in two concentric circles relating his various adventures. The center of each set of circles is a scene in which Odysseus is asleep. The two sets with the *Nekyia* between them are themselves surrounded by twin episodes of two-day storms, and the whole structure rotates around an axis of an antithetical symmetry consisting of the warring Kikones at one end (at the beginning of his *nostos*) and the hospitable Phaeakians on the other (the present). This complex balanced arrangement is illustrated in Figure 1.

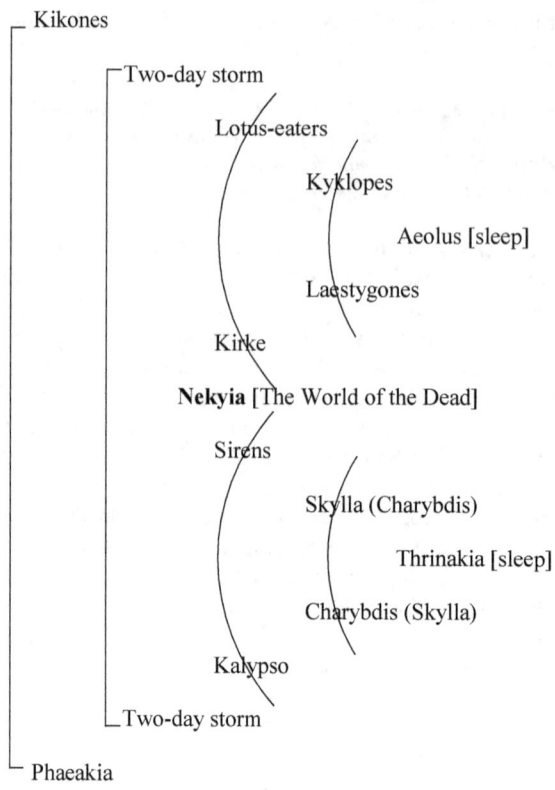

Figure 1. Ring composition in the Apologoi (after Most, 1989, p. 490).

Such a precise architectonic powerfully dramatizes the hero's central death anxiety (journey to the underworld, the disasters resulting from his falling asleep) and the numerous adversities related to it, adversities that threaten to frustrate his efforts to "return home" (*nostos*).

If we look more carefully at the nature of the calamities that Odysseus recounts we note that they are basically of two types, organized in a symmetrical pattern. In the episodes at the outer ring of each of the two sets, he speaks of the misfortunes that he suffered as a result of seduction and helpless submission (the "lovely-haired" goddess Kalypso who kept him in her island for ten years; the Sirens and their enchanting song; Kirke the dreadful bewitching goddess; the Lotus-Eaters whose honey-sweet fruit brings oblivion and total passivity). In the inner rings of each set, on the other hand, he narrates his dreadful experiences in facing devouring, man-eating monsters (Charybdis, Skylla, the Laestrygones, and the Kyklopes). These are basic primitive anxieties (passivity, seduction, oral aggression) which need to be integrated through speech in the course of psychological development in order to lessen the suffering they cause and to contain their destructive potential.

Our question is: If humans are compelled, so to speak, to make songs of their suffering, why is this so? What is achieved by this transfer (*meta-phora*) of pain to words? What does *aoidé* do? What is the experiential "gain" in this metaphoric process?

In the events that we just saw taking place in the Phaeakian court, which are centered on story-telling, we can make a number of observations. There is the striking difference between the response of the court's nobles to the Demodokos' tales and the response of the stranger: The former find the story pleasing (*terpos*) but the latter silently sheds bitter tears (*threnos*). This understandable difference, expressing the fact that for the courtly audience these are words telling of another's sorrows but for the stranger they are still raw flesh, calls attention to the verbal "muteness" of the stranger at this point. And as long as he cannot speak about it, as long as his pain remains unspoken, he remains nameless and his 'speech' is only bodily (tears). Our interest lies in how the stranger, who still lacks an identity, is being changed as he listens to his misfortunes being told by *another* (i.e., the court's bard). The immediate effect of this, as we saw, is the release of tears and his groaning – the first, inarticulate, expression of his suffering. It is here, with these inarticulate sounds, that his *Apologoi* really begin.

The stranger's grief is portrayed by Homer through the use of the remarkable simile of the spouse being torn away from the fallen dead body that she was once united with. This is the pain of profound loss, of an amputation of one's own body as it were, and the stranger's corresponding bodily reaction (tears, burying himself in his cloak to make his body disappear) indicates that he is unable, at this point, to deal with this loss on any level other than that of his wounded physical body. When the story-teller's words become too painful for him because they remind him, or rather because they re-*present* intolerable losses (of his comrades, of his former glory) the scene must drastically change: Words are abandoned and the assembly now turns to the concrete physical activity of athletic games and dancing, and, later, to the amorous tale of the union of Ares and Aphrodite. Such alternation seems, for the moment, necessary if the recitation is to continue. It is the stranger himself who brings an end to this interlude by asking the minstrel to return to the story of Odysseus. It would seem that once the word (*epos*) has made its appearance as an expression of the body it cannot be undone or erased; there is no way back. An historical clock has been started that cannot be stopped. The bard's words have begun the "weaving of a tissue" (*histos*) that becomes the stuff out of which an *histor*ical being, a new creature, will emerge, as the result of a radical change. Demodokos resumes the tale of the Ithakan hero, after which the nameless stranger will be able to proclaim: "I am Odysseus." And, immediately, he will continue *himself* telling his own story (*historia*) with the art of the bard and the words of the Other that have now become his *own*.

So, to attempt an answer to our question: The "maternal" word-song allows mourning to take place (allows the unspeakable loss to be mourned) which leads to the toleration of the aloneness of the "I" and the foundation of identity. This, in turn, makes self-narration possible, as well as the construction of a self-definition in an historical perspective: *auto-bio-graphein* ("the tracing of one's own life"). Thus the *aoidé* sung *to* the wretched stranger who was washed off by the hostile sea onto the shores of the hospitable royal couple (birth scene) led to his transformation by turning his unspeakable pain and suffering into a tolerable and speakable personal narrative that establishes his identity and his capacity to make sense of his phantastical experiences. The 'maternal' *aoidé* achieves this through its primal metaphoric function which transforms a physical state into a psychic activity that can be put into words (*epea*), thereby making physical pain bearable.

AOIDÉ

Such insights, generated by the creative mind of a great poet, were elaborated and elucidated twenty-eight centuries later by psychoanalysts. Poets have a clear advance on matters psychic, and the prudent psychoanalyst knows well how to listen. To be noted: It is not an allegorical (of necessity dyschronic) listening to the *Odyssey* that I am proposing here, in the tradition of such attempts that started, in fact, in Antiquity and continued right up to the Renaissance. Undoubtedly, each epoch has used the Great Epics as an expression of its own concerns and dilemmas and in an attempt to derive shared cultural meaning from them. What the poet's mindset was we can only speculate; in other words, we can only have a specular response to the epic that reflects our own *Zeitgeist*. I, too, wish to use the epic – specifically, the Phaeakian episode – in a psychoanalytic perspective, as a metaphor of what we can speculate retroactively to be going on between a mother and her *infans* (or *nepios* = no *epea*, no words), that is, as a metaphor of the primary metaphoric process which enables the *infans* to acquire a name, speech and the capacity to tell stories. Admittedly, what *really* goes on at that time of development we cannot ever know, but neither is this our primary concern in analysis. As Green (2000b) pointed out, "our true object is not the infant but the *infant in the adult* [emphasis added], which may have very little to do with the question of what really happened to the patient in infancy" (p. 58). My ultimate aim, however, is to use the Phaeakian episode as a metaphor of what essentially goes on in the *hic et nunc* between analyst and analysand. Reflecting on the poet's insights, I submit, can significantly enrich our understanding of the psychoanalytic process and of object relations in general.

If, as was said above, the poetic act is the body's relocation in the non-topos of phantasy, Freud's hallucinatory wish-fulfilment is the first poetic act. Prompted by the absence of the need-satisfying object, this first ideic creation is the archetype of thought, a poetic proto-thought. Yearning for the lost object and wishing to re-establish contact with it is, of course, the core theme of the

Odyssey (*nostos*). Bion (1962a) explicitly placed the object's unavailability at the origin of thought, as when a pre-conception mates with a frustration. The result of frustration is pain and physical distress that threatens disorganization. The capacity to forestall this by resorting to hallucination and phantasy is not inborn but requires a special kind of input from the outside. Enter mother-*aoidos* and her phantastical stories. But – *pace* Bion – before she can assist her infant (through her reverie) to form a *thought* out of an intolerable bodily frustration, she must first assist it to form an organized experience of its body, a body which only then could manifest the "dispositions" or expectations (Bion's "pre-conceptions," Kant's "empty thoughts") that would eventually generate thoughts. The journey is not from inborn pre-conceptions to thoughts, but from the body as a raw datum to thought. Such is the complete itinerary of the *metaphora*.

The mentalization of the body and the emergence of the psyche consists in the staging and playing out of the body's scenarios on an analogical level (thinking). What is obvious is that such a metaphoric transfer becomes possible only in the dyadic context (the *aiodos* and the "nameless stranger") of what will become an object relation. The details of *how* this transfer – what we have called the primary metaphor – occurs have been skillfully elaborated by Piera Aulagnier (Castoriades-Aulagnier, 1975, Aulagnier, 1984). Her rich theorizing on this process cannot be reviewed here, but her model is most helpful in understanding the essence of the events that unfold in Books 8-13 of the *Odyssey*. Schematically, we might say that Demodokos' *aoidé* is the maternal *acte de parole* that transforms Odysseus, who until this point is an *ombre parlée*, into an *ombre parlante*, able to recount his own story. The court bard's narration is, in effect, a *mise-en-scène* of the guest's (newly-arrived/newborn at the shores of the hospitable royal couple) physical sufferings and, further, their *mise-en-sens* that endows them with meaning and renders them thinkable and speakable. Aulagnier emphasizes the violence of this process (due to the non-isomorphic character of the transfer from the body to the word) and we saw this in Odysseus' pain while listening to the bard. Here I would like to stress its creative (*poiein, poietic*) aspect that gives rise to the speaking subject. The journey from the physical to the psychic body entails the creation of a new entity (in a sense, *ex nihilo*) which accounts for the latter's enigmatic character.

A crucial component of the process and its pivotal moment is the *threnos* (mourning). The bard-mother's "narrative" (not to be equated with her verbal narrative only), in its attempt to replace the body with thought and word, initiates mourning for a body lost, left behind. Thoughts reach us only through sorrow, says Proust (*A la recherche du temps perdu*). It must be also noted that the painful task is further complicated by the fact that the word cast on the bodily state is brought from *elsewhere* (*epipherein*), from the Other, and is, thus, "alien" (Aristotle, *Poetics*, 1457b 8) to the body, wherein lies the source of violence in the act of speech.

It would appear that mourning is indispensable for the production of thought and as such it can be termed *the work of thought*. It is the necessary work that must be done by the nascent "I" in the course of separating from a narcissistic fusional body (mother-infant), and in leaving behind a fused body-mind state. The narcissistic wholeness that is left behind is mourned as a dead body (cf. the simile of the spouse torn away from *her* dead body, the body she was united with). Plato has stressed the link between the activity of thinking (philosophy) and death (*Phaedo* 67e 4-5). The critical issue here, as Bion (1962b) among others has taught us, is the emerging "I"'s capacity to tolerate loss.

The infant's confused, chaotic bodily experience is transferred to (*meta-pherein*) the mother's mind to be elaborated there and transformed into thought, which, at first, is the thought of the Other (i.e., belonging to the Other). This is the primal poetic metaphorization, in which the body of the *infans* becomes a psychic event first in the psyche of the mother – an event that she can then "narrate," as Demodokos does. It may well be that the foundation of the so-called epistemophilic instinct is the desire of the thought of the Other, from the infant's side, as it is the thought of the Other's desire, from the mother's side. But in this process the *infans* unavoidably loses its body in order to gain a mind/psyche whose foundation lies outside the self. This primeval loss becomes the prototype of all subsequent losses.

The chief outcome of the separation from the body and the formation of thought (as a substitute/representation of the body) is the emergence of a sense of identity – of an "I" which is differentiated and different from the original fusional bodily *matrix* – and, also, the concomitant appearance of an object which is separate and Other. Thus, the axis of the dialectic "body-mind" is intersected by that of the dialectic "I-Other." This is so because, as the maternal *aoidé* "applies" words to the *infans*' body (giving rise to mind), it inaugurates, and imposes, an inevitable separation from a body which now becomes the body of the Other. Thought and Otherness make their appearance contemporaneously, and their intimate relationship means that all thought is fundamentally alien.

Thus, a sense of identity ("I am Odysseus") is, we might say, the first product of the psyche. The "I" is (in)formed by thought. It is the subject of thought, the thinking subject. The ruptured body is now metaphorized, that is, transubstantiated into a symbol: "The form of words is on you," says Alkinoos to Odysseus, after the latter's *Apologoi* (11: 367): Odysseus has been shaped by the word, he has taken on the shape of the word.

Words as symbols disrupt *equations* (Segal, 1957), affirming the radical discontinuity between thing and word, between body and mind, which reflects the discontinuity between self and Other. But, at the same time, symbols bring together what has been severed[24] in order to re-establish a bond between what are now separate entities. The symbol is an attempt to heal the rupture but

---

[24] The Greek *symbolon* was a fragment of an inscribed tablet broken in two, each fragment being kept by each of two separated friends and then brought together in recognition of their friendship.

it does not abolish the gap; it is the result of a metaphoric process and provides a link across differences (Aristotle, *Poetics* 1459a 7). The "I" will always carry the memory of its heterogeneous constitution.

It is worth noting that the minstrel begins his *aoidé* in the context of the Queen's question to the enigmatic stranger "Who are you and from where?" which had remained unanswered. It would seem that Demodokos' narration is, at this point, an attempt to address the enigma of the guest's identity. This brings to mind Kristeva's (2000) view that narration always presupposes a question to which it is an answer. What is significant is that to the Phaeakians, supreme masters of metaphor, the newcomer represents a welcomed *aenigma* of an *alien name* (Aristotle). For himself, however, his identity is fractured and his body pained: His whole odyssey is his struggle to conjoin his Troy to his Ithaka, to bring together disparate parts of himself in order to construct his own *aenigma*. For the moment, the stranger is still *Outis*, as he was in the cave of the Kyklops (9: 364-366). Imprisoned there by the one-eyed monster, under the threat of being devoured by him, he had no means of surviving other than by refusing to differentiate and acquire an identity ("My name is Outis"), or by taking on a false identity (hiding under the belly of a ram to mislead the monster into thinking that he is a ram). When mother lacks "binocular vision" (Bion, 1962b, p. 14, and 1977), keeping the child captive inside her and disallowing separateness, no other means of survival is possible. The evolution towards symbolic thought and a sense of I-ness is blocked. Here, however, in the welcoming, supportive atmosphere of the Phaeakian royal couple, the minstrel's song initiates a process that will enable the nameless stranger to traverse the turbulent waters of the passage from the body to thought, to experience the overwhelming sorrow of loss associated with this and to construct his identity. Only then can he reach his destination (Ithaka) and claim his place among his fellow humans.

The subject's identity, rooted in alterity, can only be attained metaphorically. Constructed as it is of ingredients which are alien to each other, it will always harbor an enigma. Similarly, the thought of the object – and consequently the object of thought – insofar as it is the product of the metaphoric process is, also, forever enigmatic. This is fundamentally due to the non-isomorphism between thought and thing. Hence the riddle of the Sphinx: Half lion/half human, this monstrous hybrid of body and word, *presents* an enigma to the passer-by, not in what she asks but in what she *is*. The infant is not confronted with the enigma *of* the Sphinx but with the enigma *in* the Sphinx. And to this *she* has no answer either, since, as Laplanche (1987) points out, the Other's enigmatic message is a product of her own unconscious (pp. 124-126) which conveys her own version of the primal metaphor.

We recall that Teiresias had forewarned Odysseus, during the latter's voyage through the underworld, that he could only reach his destination transported "by *another*'s ship" (11: 115). This ship that will be made available to him by another is the Phaeakian ship which Homer characterizes as a "*thinking* vessel:" the vessels of the Phaeakians "discern their direction by their own mind;" "they, by themselves, understand the minds of men" (8: 556-559); they are ships that are "swift as thought" (7: 36), he says. Thus Odysseus will complete his project only with the intervention of a thinking vessel, a thought, which belongs to an Other. And his identity as a thinking subject will bear the marks of another's thought. "If a psyche is to come to know itself it must see itself through another psyche," Plato claimed (*Alkibiades* 133b 7). A creature (a creation) of metaphor, Odysseus will be the product of "the application of an alien name" and, consequently, the core of his identity will be, forever, inhabited by the Other: *Je est un autre* (Rimbaud).

And so, although the nameless newcomer to the royal palace will, in time and through his own narration, acquire a name and become the *poietes* or maker of his identity, the foundation of his identity will be *ek-topic*, de-centered. Such alienation in the construction of the "I" is due to the fact that the *infans'* experience of his body is "narrated" or "named" by mother and, of necessity, in her own somato-psychic alphabet. Thus, there is, in fact, a double alienation: What is "applied" to the *infans* is the Other's word, that is, the Other's Other. And yet it would seem that self-alienation is the condition that makes narration possible. It makes possible the narration of the self as Other and, as Homer was the first one to suggest, this leads to *terpos* (8: 44-45). The shift to the word – "flesh made word" – renders the bodily pain containable and tolerable.

The narration of the maternal *aiodos* effectuates what the Ancients called *logon didonai* (see Plato, *Republic* 534 b4). This notion signifies "giving an account," imbuing something with sense or inner meaning. But, at the same time, it indicates "giving speech," endowing an event with language, since giving an account of an event, rendering it coherent, is making it accessible to language, making it speakable. Once the *infans* is endowed with psychic language and meaning, it can, itself, "give an account" of its archaic anxieties, as Odysseus does in Books 9-13. These primitive phantasies and fears of being seduced into helpless passivity, timelessness, and dissolution, on the one hand, and being engulfed/devoured by a terrifying monster, on the other, can now be contained in narrative "rings," as it were, and made tolerable. The essential function of mother's "narration" is *logon didonai*, or, assigning meaning to the raw sensory experiences (body) so that disorganization is avoided. The creation of meaning is the ultimate aim of metaphor.[25]

Students of Homer have long been puzzled by two features in the Scherian episode of the *Odyssey* which, they feel, raise difficult questions with regard to the epic's narrative economy, creating serious irregularities in narrative convention and coherence (de Jong, 1995, pp. 486-7; see also Fenik, 1974, pp. 5-60). Various solutions to the puzzle have been suggested but disagreement and debate persist to this day – and so does the mystery relative

---

[25] The notion that poetry, through metaphor, seeks to make suffering meaningful is in contradiction with Adorno's view that to write poetry after Auschwitz is barbaric (Adorno, 1967, 1973).

to the dramatic function of these two "peculiarities" in the story. The first one has to do with the remarkable delay in Odysseus' stating his identity: the Queen asks him in 7: 238 to say who he is but his reply comes only in 9: 19! This violates the rules of dramatic as well as social propriety, exclaim the nineteenth century philologists, since there is no practical reason motivating the guest to conceal his identity at this point (as there *is*, for example, upon his arrival in Ithaka); in fact, it would have been to his advantage to say who he is right away and thereby secure the Phaeakians' hospitality. *Ergo*, it is claimed, all the intervening lines, namely, the remaining of Book 7 and all of Book 8, ought to be deleted as spurious! They are interpolations to the original version by a subsequent inferior poet (Kirchhoff, 1879; Schadewaldt, 1966, p. 256; Wilamowitz-Möllendorf, 1884, p. 133). There has been one lone voice, however, proposing a different view: Mattes (1958) suggests that the stranger, "in his own *consciousness*," at the point of his arrival at Scheria, is *not* Odysseus but a man plagued by inhuman suffering and as such has no name yet. Before he acquires a name, Mattes (1958) concludes, "a lot must take place, and precisely that which is described in Book 8" (p. 140), that is, the minstrel's narration, the stranger's reaction, and so forth. Our explanation goes along the same lines. We hold that the stranger does not declare his identity earlier because *he does not have one yet*. He needs the *aoidé* to lead him to it.

The second question troubling literary critics is: Why does Odysseus embark on the lengthy recounting of his sufferings at that particular moment in the story, that is, right after the court's minstrel's song about him and the establishment of his identity? And, also, how can we understand the kind of misfortunes that he describes? Here, again, a psychoanalytic perspective recognizes the underlying coherence in such developments of the narrative. Only after his sorrows have been *spoken* by the singer, "translated" into a verbal form, is Odysseus capable of becoming an "epic" hero, that is, endowed himself with meaningful speech (*epea*) and with the capacity to tell his story. Before this point, *he couldn't*. And, it seems, he couldn't wait to put his pain in words (9:37). As for the form of his misadventures, we discern here universal archaic fears/wishes, the basic elements of which are reminiscent of Lewin's triad of "eat - be eaten - sleep" (Lewin, 1946, 1973).

In the Postscript to *Group psychology and the analysis of the ego*, Freud (1921, p. 133) speculates about the emergence of the individual from the group to become the first epic poet. In a momentous advance that he "achieved in his imagination," the individual "freed himself from the group" and told a story that was a true story disguised as a lie. The heroic myth recounted by the individual was, according to Freud, the murder of the primal father. In the schema proposed here, suggested by the Homeric sequence of events, it would appear what the first epic narrative related instead the *beginning* of all suffering (the *pematos arche*), and this was the *loss of the primal object*. This violent event resulted in untold sorrows, primordial anxieties, and stubborn attempts to re-possess the object that was lost. The lost object is Helen, Chryseis, Briseis, Penelope, or Ithaka. The chief outcome of all this, as we have seen, is the construction of the hero's identity. The child's first narrative seeks to respond to the question "Who am I?" and recounts the original rupture of the fusional one-ness with mother and the subsequent attempts to create a metaphoric link that will give rise to the individual's identity as a now separate and inherently alienated subject. The narrative of the heroic myth is always an odyssey: a grievous scission and the unending efforts to undo it or repair it. Freud focused on a *later* version of this (oedipal) that disguises the truth of mother's (Jokasta's) primal violence to her infant.

Returning now to the *logon didonai* of the maternal "narrative," we note that Demodokos' song in Book 8 comes after the painful events that it recounts have taken place. This "after" has important consequences. Homer's *opisso* (afterwards) situates the *aoidé* as coming later, after the human suffering (*Iliad*, VI: 357). The body is "left behind" to become a story that can be told, as in the simile of the spouse's mourning in the *Odyssey*. But by "leaving the body behind" and mourning for it, there appears a *fossa*, a gap between the body and its thought. This is the space that will be occupied by time, the space in which a sense of time will emerge. Time is the product of the discontinuity and heterogeneity of the two poles of the metaphoric process. The sense of time that will arise from this gap will make a historicized narration of the self possible.

Put differently: Like Minerva's owl (Hegel, 1967), thought comes always *after* the somatic fact, with a delay (cf. the psychoanalytic principle of *après coup*). It is inaugurated by the (m)other who, then, "applies" it (*epipherein*) to her infant's body. The double discontinuity of alterity and heterogeneity opens up a potential space, and it is here that a sense of time makes its appearance. Goethe's Faust, we recall, is not satisfied with the biblical "In the beginning was the Word (*logos*)." No! He asserts, "In the beginning was the Act" (Goethe, 1962, line 1237). The diachronic hiatus between the original somatic "act" and its reflection in and by the word generates the sense of time. *Chronos* (time) derives from *Kronos*, which comes from *krainein* ("to accomplish," "to carry out," "to fulfill"). The original soma, the soma of the unconscious, is a-temporal. In accomplishing, in carrying out, the metaphoric translocation that transforms it into a *psychic* soma, it becomes temporalized. Time is the product accomplished by the process of the primal metaphor. Now the temporalized psychic soma is endowed with an identity which is historical. The "I" is constituted through its historization. This means, however, that the "I" is, of necessity, *ek-static* in the Heideggerian sense, de-centered in time. Poetic memory (*Mnemosyne*), like analytic memory, seeks to re-establish links with the body "left behind." By so doing, it permits a re-orientation of the "I", which can now recollect rather than re-live his *drama* (*dran* = to act). This is what Odysseus does in his *Apologoi*.

Since the *aoidé* comes after the body and its suffering, "leaving the body behind" as it transforms it into word, it can be said to be a sort of monument of the body. And since, ultimately, it records the memory of a body lost (the body of the original mother-infant fusion), the *aoidé* is indeed a funerary monument "for those yet to come."

There is a moving story in the *Odyssey*, the story of Elpenor who died an inglorious death in the island of Kirke and was left there unburied. His phantom pleads with Odysseus, during the latter's descent to the underworld, to give him a proper burial, to heap up a mound for him on the shore of the grey sea and to fix upon it his oar as a "monument (*sema*) of an unfortunate man, so that those yet to come may hear of me" (11: 75-77). *Aoidé* is an oar to navigate loss; it is always inscribed, as it were, on a funeral *stele*. It is a *sema*, a sign in the linguistic sense, recalling objects lost, bodies that have become Other. This points to the word's primal poetic function, as a tomb of lost objects. In the *Iliad*, the only *aiodos* present is in Hektor's funeral: "They laid him [Hektor] on a carved bier and around him they set singers leading the lament" (XXIV:720-721). The centrality of mourning in the poetic act is brought out here.

Thus, the maternal *aoidé* is a birth-song, a song that leads to the infant's identity ("I am Odysseus"), but it is also a dirge, a reminder that the identity of humans is born of losses. *Aoidé* is, ultimately, a *logon didonai* of death.

A METAPHOR OF THE PRIMAL METAPHOR

The Phaeakian episode provides us with a paradigm of the emergence and development of the psyche. This is obviously a model constructed by the adult mind after the fact and, of necessity, with the contribution of phantasy. It is a psychic elaboration by analysand and analyst alike, a narrative that attempts to answer the fundamental questions of being, not-being, and origin. According to this model, the infant's unorganized bodily sensations become "metaphorized" in the mother's mind, flesh becoming thought and word in her mouth, in order to "fly out"[26] and return to the infant where the word will be embodied again, but in a radically transformed state. This is the quintessence of "sublimation." Such mentalization of the body is only attainable in the context of the primal dyad with its quality of "dual unity;" it leads to an identity based on separateness and is the necessary condition for object relations. We have called the trans-fer of the bodily to the mental "primal metaphor," and claimed it to be the fundamental principle governing human psychological development. The process is intrinsically *poietic* in so far as it leads to the creation of a new category or level of being which is heterogeneous with respect to its origins to which, however, it will always be enigmatically related. Human psychological growth, in its poetic dimension, aims towards *meta-phorein*, which is the leap of humanization that manifests itself in the capacity to make and tell stories that organize primitive anxieties and lessen the pain of loss, expressing them in the "poeticity" (Jakobson, 1987) of the first language of humanity.

The metaphoric project is lifelong, owing to the asymptotic character of the two elements to be linked. Man is condemned to an endless chain of attempts to construct an answer to the metaphoric enigma, none of which can

---

[26] *See* Homer's frequent formulaic expression: "[She] addressed [him] in flying words."

be adequate. We might, thus, speak of an immanent metaphoric *drive* which can be taken as a metaphor for life itself. Aristotle implied something like this when he stated that life is the *energeia* of thinking (*Metaphysics* Bk XII, 1072b 27).

The psychoanalytic process itself can be seen as a ring in this endless chain, a segment in man's interminable series of attempts at self-transformation. The primal metaphor can, thus, be considered to be the essence of the psychoanalytic process itself.

We have seen, by listening to Homer, that poetry can exert a "therapeutic" effect on its listeners by rendering primitive anxieties and their associated pain more tolerable through their containment in and by the word (Books 8-13), and we have suggested that poetry achieves this via the process of primal metaphorization. It is metaphor that is responsible for poetry's "therapeutic" effect. Metaphor brings this about by carrying out a "re-description of reality" (Ricoeur, 1975) on the basis of new meaning engendered as the result of a transformative interaction between metaphor's two referents (Black, 1962). This, ultimately, effectuates a translocation of pain and suffering from the body to the mental and to the symbolic register from where it can be narrated.

The healing effect of poetry has been stressed by several authors. Akhtar (2000), for example, believes that poetry "facilitates the mentalization of the non-verbal substrate of the psyche" (p. 236) and "can have an impact upon pain that is akin to a psychoanalytic intervention" (p. 239). Philosophers reflecting on the inherent value of art in general have long recognized the beneficial effects that the aesthetic experience can have on the human psyche and its growth. They speak of art bringing about a "reconciliation of opposite tendencies," "developing the ability to put oneself in the place of others," "drawing men together, forming bonds between them," and so on (Beardsley, 1981, pp. 500-583). With specific reference to poetry and metaphor, Richards (1970) argues that the poetic experience in particular leads to an integration and a harmonization of impulses with pervasive benefit to mental health.

It is our contention that the beneficial effects produced by psychoanalysis stem from its efforts to promote and enhance the primal metaphoric process. This would mean that there is an *underlying poetic dimension* in the psychoanalytic enterprise in its aim towards psychic growth. Although the metaphoric work may be more prominent in the analysis of psychotic-borderline states and in psychosomatic disorders, we suggest that the metaphoric project constitutes the infrastructure of *all* analyses. According to such a view, what the analytic process endeavors is to create new and more coherent narratives of the analysand's unconscious bodily phantasy [see Isaacs' (1948) definition of phantasy]. It aims at constructing new psychic scenaria of bodily events and giving them voice.[27] The analytic intervention finds, thus, its

---

[27] It should be mentioned that part of the material to be transformed originates in the analysand's mother, and this so for the following reason: the first attempt to mentalise the infant's body was made by her, but her narratives contained unelaborated,

place as part of the continuous lifelong metaphoric process undertaken by the "I" in its effort to speak meaningfully of its body states, a project that is never completed.

We conclude that the Phaeakian episode can be taken as a metaphor of the primal metaphoric process as the latter unfolds not only in psychic development but also in psychoanalysis. Homer's "theory of poetry" provides us with a metaphor for a theory of the psychoanalytic process, a metaphor for a theory which is itself metaphoric. Human growth, it seems, can only occur and be spoken of metaphorically.

---

repressed body components of *her own* (Laplanche, 1987, p. 125) which had never been "translated" into psychic terms. The infant inherits parts of mother's unconscious body which provide the nucleus for the infant's and later the adult's unconscious - a body of unconscious phantasy still waiting to be mentalised.

Chapter Three

The return of Odysseus
Questions of time, space, and creative discovery

The friendly Phaeakians, sailing their swift ship, "swift as a feather or as a thought," have brought the old traveler home and have laid him sleeping on the soft sand of his native shores (*Odyssey*, 13). Sweet sleep has fallen upon his eyelids, "deep, most sweet sleep, most like to death." The grief, the wars, the losses, the pain of the ruthless waves are all gone now, forgotten. He sleeps calmly, motionless, at the edge of the murmuring sea.

Soon the morning star heralds the rose-fingered dawn of a new day. He opens his eyes. He is frightened. He jumps up: "Woe is me! To the land of what mortals have I come? Are they cruel and savage, or are they kind to strangers?" The land, the landscape of which he has been dreaming for so long, is *not* what his sees now with his eyelids open. This is not a place that he recognizes. It is "of a different kind," says Homer (*alloeidea*).

And so life begins, on each awakening from sleep, from fantasy, always re-experiencing that primordial moment of the first encounter with an unfamiliar outside world following birth. Two images on either side of the eyelids, dream and external reality, two worlds, pre-natal and post-natal, worlds that are discrepant and clash. The perception of the outside is that of a hostile place, and the tendency to repudiate it in order to maintain sameness remains forever strong: in order to maintain sameness, that is, in the service of timeless Thanatos.

In the *Odyssey,* this scene in Book 13, at the culmination of the hero's homecoming, is of the highest dramatic quality and marks the passage from what we might consider as Part One to Part Two of the Poem. It is this "passage" and what it represents in psychic life that will occupy us here. This is the juncture of two realities, the moment when two radically different worlds come into contact, a moment of confusion and terror. Another Odysseus, a new Odysseus, is to be born, in another world. And the two worlds are now permanently disconnected: The ship that brought Odysseus to Ithaka from the hospitable island of Scheria – the *link* between the two worlds – has been turned into a rock on its way back, rooted to the sea floor, petrified for eternity. Odysseus' task – the fundamental human task – will be, now, to construct the missing link, or, rather, to begin an interminable *series* of attempts to construct links that bridge the two worlds, without ever quite succeeding.

The pressing question: Was it all a dream? On the inner side of the eyelids? A nightmare? Troy, Polyphemos, the Laestrygones, Kirke: Could it be that they never *really* existed? That Odysseus now wakes up after a terrifying dream of war and persecution? Or, is *this* a dream? He never really returns to Ithaka's cherished shores: This is only a cruel dream of wish-fulfillment, a fantasy! (The Phaeakian ship that brought him to Ithaka was like a "swift thought," a magic ship that charts its course by itself "knowing the minds and thoughts of men"). Or, further still, is it *all* an uninterrupted dream as Odysseus continues a deceptive, never-ending slumber? This last possibility is always tempting to humans since, here, no links that bring into relation two clashing categorically different universes need be constructed. But this endless Hypnos is in the service of Thanatos, as was mentioned above. Eros, on the other hand, drives consciousness to experience gaps in being and to strive to bridge them over.

The Poet cannot settle the question but he faces it. Blindly. Which made Heidegger assert that the poet speaks the sacred voice of Being. And because Being is the simultaneous affirmation of non-Being, the poet's words are always "flying words" (*epea pteroenta*), creatures in transition, hovering over worlds in transition. And so, Odysseus' sleep is no uninterrupted slumber but lies at the root of the tragic. The Homeric Epics are, unquestionably, proto-tragedy.

But let us look again at the scene of Odysseus lying on Ithaka's native shore and recall Winnicott (1971):

> The sea is the mother, and onto the seashore the child is born. Babies come out of the sea and are spewed out upon the land... So now the seashore was the mother's body, after the child is born and the mother and the now viable baby are getting to know each other (p. 95)

The Homeric scene is, ultimately, a birth scene. It is the birth of a, as yet, nameless, speechless (*nepios*, line 237) child, in an, as yet, unknown, nameless (*noonymos*, line 239) and unfamiliar land. Odysseus' *nekyia* journey to the world of the Shadows finds its converse counterpart here in his *geneté*, in his archaic passage from the primordial Sea to Land.

Frightened on account of the discontinuity of his experience ("all things looked strange and of a different appearance to him"), disoriented, a stranger to what has been his maternal soil, Odysseus is lamenting his sort, "creeping on the shore of the fluttering sea, moaning deeply" and wishing he had remained in the hospitable island from which he has come (line 204). But soon his protectoress (*phylax*) appears disguised as a shepherd. She is the first human that Odysseus meets on this lonely shore – a human, but a goddess! Athena, we are told, looks after him, being "always by his side, never doubting him, never questioning" (lines 300, 339). She is always there to be *found*, "taking on all sorts of different forms" (line 313). In short, she has all the attributes of the Winnicottian mother. It is precisely Athena's capacity to take on different forms, thereby softening the sharp impact of an immutable, alien Other and Different, that is the essence of her protectiveness. And it is, above all, at this moment of his arrival at his native but unfamiliar shore that he most needs her. And she will not fail him. She casts a morning *mist* that covers everything, the newcomer, the bays and cliffs, the goddess herself. All outlines are muted, faded, boundaries are fluid and objects can take on different identities, depending on how they are perceived by the newly-arrived stranger. If objects are to acquire form they will have to be born out of formlessness.

And the *play* (Winnicott) begins. Odysseus starts recounting a fantastical story about how he came to this shore (cf. children's birth theories), the "bright-eyed" goddess listens patiently, stroking him with her hand, smiling with pleasure at his inventiveness, enjoying the tale, playfully scolding him, herself playing her own fantastical role of the 'shepherd.' This mutuality in fantasy, in defying a reality that is imposed from without, is what joins them together, what joins mother and *infans*, and what will permit them eventually to separate.

When the right time comes Athena slowly scatters the mist so that objects and subjects gradually become distinct. Ithaka now no longer lacks a name, and the newly-arrived stranger no longer lacks words (*nepios* = *infans*) or an identity. Odysseus rejoices and kisses the "life-giving earth," but knows that now great toils and difficult tasks are awaiting him, tasks that he cannot avoid. Ithaka is no longer a dream, a yearning. The first and most treacherous reef, however, has been avoided. For the moment at least, since the dangerous straights of Skylla and Charybdis, the seductive chant of the Sirens will be encountered again and again in the course of life and will have to be navigated with uncertain degrees of success. Odysseus will always have to chart a course between the Skylla of repudiating external, "hostile" reality and remaining forever a prisoner of phantasy, and the Charybdis of repudiating the dream and phantasy, thereby remaining a prisoner of rationality and a slave to an alienating sterile outer reality. Both of these alternatives are attempts to disavow the Different and maintain the Same. Both are versions of Thanatos.

Re-finding the lost object (Ithaka), or rather, re-creating it in a new version that bears a relation of *correspondence* to the original but is not *identical* to it, giving it a name and, concomitantly, acquiring a name and a distinct subject-hood, fills the nascent self with a primordial joy and a sort of primitive, spontaneous boundless gratitude. Odysseus on the shores of Ithaka hails the daughters of Zeus, the nymphs of the sacred Cave, and offers them gifts. For the infant, this is a crucial moment on the road to humanization as it indicates that the long and tortuous process of differentiation between self and Other is well on its way, since feelings of gratitude are based on the recognition that the self has been given something that comes from the "not-me." As long as objects are "subjective," this is not possible.

At the end of a good (or "good-enough") play between mother and child (which, of course, goes on for years) – a "play" of which the writer and *metteur-en-scene*, but, also, the spectator is really the child, yet a play whose success depends largely on mother's "theatrical" skill – the child is left with a treasure. The child will be enriched by the characters it has created and especially by their "disobedience" and unpredictability. But most importantly, the self will be enriched by the internalization of a benign and friendly environment (not one which is "cruel and savage") and by the introjection of a capacity to transform persecutory terror into manageable and tolerable anxiety. This is the gift of the daughter of Zeus/mother. The treasure is now taken in by Odysseus, "into the innermost recess of the sacred Cave" (line 363), to be stored there safely for times of need, for future times when primitive fright and disorientation re-appear. This inner space is potent owing to the fact that it is where the "divine" (fantasy) meets with the human: note the *two* entrances of the cave in the tale.

The meeting of the spiritual and the material in the human psyche finds expression in that uniquely human capacity for *imagined action* that we call "thought." Alkmaion of Kroton (6th century BCE) was the first to point out that their independence from the concrete perception of the physical world is what distinguishes humans from other animals; it is what allows them to shape external reality. So now, Odysseus and Athena[28], jointly, will "weave a plan" (line 303), a narrative for future action. This *mythos* (line 374), oriented towards outer reality, towards action and the future, contrasts with the fantastical narrative *mythos* of the past, the soliloquy of an insular self that Odysseus ingeniously made up when he first encountered Athena (line 254). The play, here, of thought is more evolved and complex than the play of fancy as it takes into account the contradictory duality of inner and outer reality and, also, time. And after they "weave their myth," sitting down by the trunk of the sacred olive tree, they part: "they break off" or "divide," says Homer (line 439). They *separate*.

Homer has been the educator of generations, from early Antiquity up to the nineteenth century and, perhaps, even right through to our present "post-modern" era. He has served as the alphabet, we might say, of Western culture, providing the *vowels* of the very way we think about ourselves, about the world around us, and about the relation between the two.[29] Here, I wish to use this scene of Book 13 of the *Odyssey* – a turning point in the epos – as a sort of vowel "semanteme" to explore questions of the origin of our sense of time and of space and of their implication for creative discovery. The scene, as we have seen, portrays the archetypical moment of the coming into contact of two states of being, namely, sleeping/dreaming and wakefulness, and echoes the original passage from pre-natal to post-natal life. It poignantly highlights the

---

[28] Athena, born out of Zeus' head, is a creature of thought, hence, the goddess of wisdom. It is mother's capacity to symbolize that will allow the child to develop his own capacity.

[29] The Homeric Epics were composed in the eight century BCE, around the time when the Greek alphabet was being constructed by adding vowels to the Phoenician alphabet. There is evidence that suggests that the Greek alphabet was invented in order to render meter in the writing of poetry.

fundamental human task, never fully accomplished, of integrating these two states while keeping them separate, and points to the stark discontinuity, the irrevocable gap between them, as well as to the various inventive manoeuvres for dealing with this primordial traumatic experience.

TIME, SPACE

While Freud (1925) sought the origin of our sense of time in the oscillating cathexis of the system Pcpt-Cs, Melanie Klein (1948) advanced that it is the change from intrauterine to extrauterine life that constitutes the "prototype of periodicity," and believed this to be at the root of time sense (p. 103). Following Winnicott's metaphor of the baby coming out of the sea, spewed out upon the land and born onto the seashore, we shall search for the foundation of our sense of time in this sandy region, at the fluid boundary between sea and land. Roots in the sand? Psychic time is a most unstable and mutable entity.

I am of the view that the import of infant observation research has its limits in its applicability to adult analysis. Thus, it may be in the absence of scientific evidence, but in response to a certain kind of psychoanalytic listening that I allow myself to imagine primary states of an original fusion, of an objectless all-encompassing merge between mother and infant. This means that, according to a chronological time dialectic of progression—regression, we can imagine an oscillation, after birth, between states of absolute union with mother's body (pre-natal) alternating with states of differentiation and separateness. The back-and-forth movement between these states may be rapid and the cycle of short duration during the first weeks and months of extrauterine life. With age, as we know, the cycle normally lengthens but never disappears. I propose to consider *this* the "prototype of periodicity" and to suggest that an inchoate sense of time arises in the oscillation between states of fusion and states of separateness, emerging out of the gap in the transition from one to the other, this gap being the basic interval of time. Clearly, this is not a scientific hypothesis intended to be tested, verified or falsified, or even considered to be testable. But it may be a schema of some clinical utility, especially in those situations that we summarily designate as "borderline." It may, in fact, be considered itself as a tale, one of those jointly constructed by the analyst and the analysand in their effort to be together separately.

Herakleitos (Kirk and Raven, 1971) the "obscure", or the "riddler" as he was known in Antiquity, held that Time is a child playing, playing draughts (*pessoi*), and that the child is sovereign. Now, regarding play, a lot of creative thought has been devoted to it since Freud's (1920) *Fort-Da*. We know that playing draughts requires *two* players, as is the case of our two players of Book 13. But what are those two really doing in their play? Well, mother and child are intensely absorbed in the task of building a bridge, as it were, a bridge that separates what was fused, a bridge that links what is separated. The two are "thrown" into the situation, to use a Heideggerian concept, and the decisive issue – decisive for the future of the infant, that is – is the *degree and quality of overlap between their respective rhythms* in their particular and unique way of managing the fusion-differentiation cycle. The role of the mother, as we know, is primary here. The infant's rhythms are, at this point, essentially biological, while hers are psycho-biological. There is no need to go over Winnicott's epoch-making observations once more. What needs to be stressed, perhaps, is the element of unpredictability, of chance, in the living out of their relationship, because this is the building block of time and creativity. It is quite probable that the *pessoi* of Herakleitos' child were played with dice. Chance introduces discontinuity and it would appear that the infant's primary challenge is to find a way of dealing with that. Mother enters into the picture. She is to be *found* by the infant. By chance. And the construction of the bridge begins. She "holds time," Winnicott (1971) tells us. She does this both by re-appearing and "mending" a faded image in the infant's mind after a brief absence, and by *not* disappearing after she has been attacked and destroyed (by "surviving"). She holds time by en*during*, by ensuring that *no change* occurs. Unlike physical time, psychic time is founded on no change! And this is the root of the paradox, because mother, in re-appearing unchanged, unaffected by the infant's attacks – thereby providing a template for continuity – introduces the most fundamental change in the individual's life: The original mother-infant union is splintered into two *separate* beings, and a link is being constructed across the gap. The mother as object, as independent autonomous object, must now be brought into relation with the mother as a subjective, omnipotently controlled object. And this is Odysseus' task on Ithaka's lonely shore.

The originary moment of transition from intrauterine to extrauterine existence, with its explosive tension at the point of contact, at the interface between fusion and separateness, is re-lived not only on awakening from sleep or from daydreaming, but also at the end of each analytic session, when lucidly imagining death, etc. Two categorically different and distinct states come into contact. In the case of awakening, as in our scene of Book 13, we may say, schematically, that the dreamt object collides with the perceived object because the two are discordant. The perceived object is different but not separate yet. It is experienced as hostile and is attacked *because* it is not separate. At a time when time does not yet exist all is *now*, and instant defenses urgently come into play to deal with the discontinuity: These defenses are *splitting* and/or *merging*. The third avenue (that of constructing a bridge) is erotic, under the aegis of the Life instinct, and leads to living (and to dying), but is much more difficult because it brings into play the Other. If things work out the result will be the toleration of *two* worlds, separate but related and relating to each other. They are similar but not the same; they are not *identical* (de M'Uzan, 1977, pp. 83-97).

Awakening to perceive a world which is different and distinct from, but related to the world created by the dreamer is, as we know, a major developmental achievement and one which is never fully or permanently attained. Eventually, the maturing individual awakens to *remember* her dream. She awakens and she remembers that she awakened. She can now tell her dream to someone *else* who is somewhere *else* than the place of the dream, rather than talking to herself in the dream and dreaming that she is awake. The dream is tolerated as a double, a counterpart of the external world and as a creation of the individual. The seminal work of Clifford Scott (1975) must be acknowledged here. Time emanates, we might say, from the interaction of the two worlds. It is what the bridge that links them conveys. It makes its appearance at the dawn of psychic life, as the world of fantasy and dream begin to be differentiated from the externally perceived world. Plato suggested that the psyche is born of the mingling of the Same with the Different and that it is, accordingly, an "intermediate" structure composed of both (*Timaeus*). This would point to an essential temporality in the structure of the psyche. But for all this to happen we need the primordial medium of the *mist* and a caring object that can "take any form." This will make difference tolerable, it will permit an interplay between union and separateness, and will make possible the "weaving" of stories and of histories. "Tertiary processes," described by Green (2000a), will come into play here to construct the time bridge, and to create a space for psychic living – provided that "mother is holding the situation in time" until that function can be introjected and placed securely inside, as in Odysseus' cave. The compulsive repetitiveness of biological rhythms and the cyclical biological time that is based on them will, in time, be superseded by the *spiral* course of psychic time associated with the capacity for thought and the process of humanization.

We are, thus, led to consider psychic time as a phenomenon of transition. A transitional phenomenon? A creation arising in the intermediate area between fusion and separateness, between two "nows" where the second "now" is the same but different from the first, between the "now" of birth and the "now" of death. Time: the child of discontinuity, a concoction coming out of the same cauldron as cultural phenomena. Not a cultural phenomenon itself but bearing an underlying affinity to cultural phenomena. Ricoeur (1988) has given us an impressive analysis of the relation between time and narration, narration being the vehicle of cultural evolution. And so has Aulagnier (1984) with her concept of *autohistorisation*.

If psychic time, with respect to its origins, shares the characteristics of transitional phenomena, then its illusory, fluid, indefinite and multiform character, its inherent nature as *temps éclaté* (Green, 2000a) can be understood on that basis. Aristotle's statement is striking in this context: Time, he claims, is an equivocal and vague thing; it is and it is not (*Physics* Book IV, Ch. 10). Thus, as an intermediary structure, psychic time provides a relief both from the relentless demands of rectilinear physical time and from the imperative of the biological time of the instinctual bodily rhythms.

It is clear from the above that the sense of time and its origins cannot be understood outside an object relations frame of reference. The "field" of time is the fusion-differentiation dialectic played out within the dual unit of the mother-infant dyad. A firm identity as a subject, a clear sense of being "I" ensues emerging out of the dual unit – an identity grounded on time and inseparable from it. Heidegger, from a different perspective, has made the point convincingly, I believe.

In a fundamental sense, however, time is the time of the Other, the time carried, at first, by the care-giving primary object and this has some profound consequences for the sense of self. If being is coterminous with time and time is the time of the Other, an inescapable element of alienation inhabits the core of the self. The "I" in being temporal is constitutionally estranged from itself, it is *ek-static*, as Heidegger would say, that is, standing outside itself. This nucleus of "objectness" or otherness in the "I" represents the condition of its existence as a subject and the condition of its capacity to enter into a relation with what is non-self.

Now, entering into a relation with the non-self is what generates meaning. Meaning, too, can only be conceived within an object relation. It is the outcome of linking on two levels: linking the subject to the object, and linking the object to the earlier *subjective* object (Winnicott, 1958). Thus, meaning can be said to unfold along two vectors, one centrifugal and the other centripetal. But, since time is born of the oscillation between fusion and separateness, this dual linking is marked by temporality. Accordingly, meaning is inherently temporal, and as such, it can only be rendered narratively. The point of note here, however, is that, as the direction of both vectors is towards the Other, outer or inner (the Other-object, or the Other-Unconscious), meaning, too, like the subject that constitutes it, is fundamentally de-centered and alienating.

Time as a "transitional" phenomenon may be polymorphous (i.e., polychronous), but it rotates around the single axis defined by the timelessness of the subjective object, at one pole, and the time of the Other, at the other. This underlying duality gives psychic time its tragic sense.

Viewing the origins of time thus, we are led to the conclusion that a sense of time and of inner continuity is primary, prior to and a precondition for the firm establishment of a sense of space and of spatial differentiation. Kant (1929) had noted that time as an inner sense cannot in itself be outwardly perceived and so it comes to be represented spatially as a line. But this spatialization of time has led to all sorts of impasses (*vide* Saint Augustine), as Wittgenstein (2009) has pointed out, and has tempted us to regard the time sense as secondary and as a derivative of space. The question that concerns us here, however, relates to *pre*-representational states and experiences. It would appear that a sense of continuity along changing states, that is, an inner sense of time, is an essential element in the cohesion and integration of the self – or, more precisely, in the first level of integration of the self – and that it is a *sine qua non* for the adequate toleration of a sense of space that permits spatial separateness. The sense of time is, thus, primary and can be said to act as a container (in Bion's sense) of space, establishing the latter's boundaries.

In the "misty" intermediate space that opens up between infant and mother, a space which is full of ambiguities and paradoxes, all forms, shapes and identities, all of life's contradictory scenarios are to be invented, created, without anyone asking why. It is the space of life's theater. Thus, Athena will dress up Odysseus as an other: "But come, I will make you unknown to all mortals. I will shrivel the handsome skin on your supple limbs, destroy the fair hair on your head, clothe you in a ragged garment ..." (lines 397ff.). This fanciful creative play will lead, in time, to rational thought and action. But for this to happen a difficult challenge must, first, be met.

There is an old Balkan legend of the construction of a bridge. Skilled masons, strong young men, would toil hard building it all day but, at night, it would collapse into a heap of rubble. Until the voice of the spirit of the river was heard: The bridge would only stand if the chief mason sacrifices his young wife at its foundation. The primary, totally satisfying, ideal object must be given up and be mourned before any genuine creation becomes possible. This is a painful process and repeated attempts would be made to disavow the gap between the ideal "subjective object" and the objective object in order to avoid the necessity of constructing a bridge between them and making the sacrifice for that. Such was the case of Nora.

Nora would lie on the couch and fantasize that she is drifting away at sea on a raft. Soon she would be asleep, frequently in the fetal position. She would wake up at some point, be disoriented, ask anxiously where she is, turn around to look at the analyst, and then promptly fall asleep again and dream that she is looking from great depths at the analyst's hazy outline coming from the other side of the water, outside the sea. She explained, in time, that on these occasions she would flood her head with an oratorio which she associated to a lullaby her mother used to sing to her and thereby "tune out" the analyst's voice, before falling asleep. She said that sleeping was "slipping" into her mother's arms, into her mother's bed. Sometimes, the oratorio asserted: "My voice is your voice." She would always insist that what the analyst had to say was an exact repetition of what she herself had already said and that she was only hearing the echo of her own voice. In sleeping, she explained, "the outside is my inside into which I go." One day she spoke of the Chinese philosopher who slept and dreamt that he was a butterfly. He laid on a flower, on a beautiful spring day, and fell asleep and dreamt that he was a philosopher. When he woke up he didn't know whether he was a philosopher dreaming he was a butterfly or a butterfly dreaming he was a philosopher. There were sessions in which she would fall asleep and dream that she came to her session and fell asleep and dreamt that she woke up and told me about it, and then she would wake up and, in a sleeping voice, tell me about it. At the end of the session as she was walking out she would give the impression of sleepwalking. Thus, her inner world was the only world for her, which she externalized on waking up and re-internalized it in the fashion of a Möbius strip. The objective external world (the Different) was summarily and unceremoniously "tuned out" and Nora lived in a fantasied state of uninterrupted fusion with her idealized primary object. She refused to give it up as the pain of loss and of mourning was intolerable. Since there was no space separating us I had the distinct feeling that she was not talking to *me*. It was as if words were not in her mouth on their way out, "flying words" towards another person.

Instead, they were concrete, material things filling her mouth like a breast. And as for her sense of time, it seemed to be non-existent: There would be times when she would get up and leave after five minutes of lying on the couch, believing that the session had ended, and other times when she would not get off the couch believing that there was no way that fifty minutes had already passed! And, of course, there would be many missed sessions which were not even noticed that they were missed because it was as if she had never left the couch. It took many years of hard work before *two* persons could be tolerated in the room.

Let us now turn to Odysseus and to a consideration of the relation between a nostalgic return to the past and the first moments of acquisition of a sense of time on the one hand, and the capacity for forward movement and the making of new discoveries, on the other.

NOSTALGIA AND EPISTEMOPHILIA

It has been a long time now that the iron sword has done its duty,
The duty of revenge carried out;
It has been a long time now that sharp arrows and spears
Have spilled the blood of strife.
Against a god and his sea
Odysseus has come back to his kingdom and to his Queen,
Against a god and the grey storm winds,
Against the war clamor of Ares.
It has been a long time now that the queen is resting
Lightly in his arms, in the love of their spousal berth.
But where is that other man
Who, in the days and nights of exile,
Like a hound wandered through the wide world
And who said that his name is No-man?
(Borges, 2000)

Yet, the "man of many ruses" was a man of many identities. Are we to believe, then, that his story ended with his return to Ithaka? Homer perhaps only *started* the tale and left us with a hint: recall Teiresias' counsel to Odysseus, in the world of the Shadows: "But when you have slain the suitors in your palace, then, taking a shapely oar, go abroad, far away until you come to men who know nothing of the sea."

The narrative remains ambiguous as to whether Odysseus' *final* home will be Ithaka.

Odysseus will leave again, for another *Odyssey*. "My native soil is foreign lands!" he will admit in Kazantzakis' *Odysseia*. He has learned that alienation is a condition of existence because it is a *conditio sine qua non* of I-ness. Time cannot be stopped, which means that *nostos* (homecoming) as a *final* destination can be achieved only in death. So when Athena, upon his landing on

Ithaka, admonishes him: "You are a stubborn man, crafty and insatiable in deceit. Not even in your own land would you stop deceiving with fraudulent tales which you love since you were a child," (13: 293-295) are we to think that his very return is one more of his ruses?

It was left for Dante (and others) to tell us of the nostalgia of the *other* Odysseus, or of Odysseus' *other* nostalgia:

> *Neither tenderness for a son, nor the compassion*
> *for an old father, nor the debt of love*
> *owed to Penelope that would make her happy*
> *could vanquish the passion that was inside me*
> *to come to experience the world,*
> *the human vices and the virtues.*
> *And so I set forth on the open sea ...*

He urges his men:

> *Brothers ... do not deny yourselves the experience*
> *of the other side of the Sun, of the world where no one lives.*
> *Think of the seed that sowed you:*
> *You were not made to live like brutes*
> *but to seek virtue and knowledge*
> (Dante, *Inferno*, Canto XXVI).

There is good reason to believe that Dante identified with Odysseus in his unyielding search for knowledge. And he condemned him to infernal punishment not for his deceitfulness, it seems, but for his hybristic, insatiable lust to know. Dante's Odysseus sails through the Pillars of Herakles, the western limits of the medieval world, and out to the unknown "sinister" open sea.

The wish to know, Freud's *Wisstrieb* (1905), has had a tortuous evolution in psychoanalytic literature. Freud related it to the sexual researches of childhood and to *Schautrieb*, Abraham (1924) linked it to orality, and Melanie Klein (1975) saw it first as a libidinal derivative but later associated it with the sadistic impulses of the early oedipal situation. But Freud (1905) was cautious: He stressed that the drive to know "cannot be classed as exclusively belonging to sexuality" (p. 194). It may derive its energy from the "drive to look" but it is not all sexual. In any event, Freud (1905) admits that the origin of the *Schautrieb* itself "is not completely intelligible" (p. 201). I think it is possible to maintain that there are non-libidinal and non-aggressive elements in an epistemophilic drive whose aim would be to seek stimulation and to work for the integration of various stimuli. It may come to be associated with libidinal or aggressive drives but is not a derivative of them.

At the other end, and in conflict with the wish to know, there is the regressive pull of the *Schlaftrieb* (Freud, 1940). Freud related this "sleep drive" to the wish to return to intrauterine existence, to a "pre-mundane state" in which relations with the external world are broken off and all interest in it ceases.

Insofar as its aim is to achieve zero tension it would be a manifestation of Thanatos.

Now, when *nostos* takes the form of a wish to return to the original state of fusion and un-differentiation then it is clearly governed by a dominant death drive, as was the case of Nora. The new and different is repudiated, experienced as hostile and attacked. Here we have the reign of the Kleinian paranoid-schizoid position. A sense of time never develops. This *nostos* is really a *nekyia*, a return to the timeless world of the dead for the sole purpose of taking up permanent residence there.

But there is also another *nostos*, one undertaken for a different purpose and which is under the dominance of Eros, the "linker." The reason for returning to the native soil, here, is in order to re-discover old discoveries, specifically the *earliest* discoveries at the very origin of consciousness, and to relate them to and integrate them with new discoveries. The Odysseus of this *nostos*, after returning to his Ithaka, will leave again for the open seas. Having acquired a sense of time he is now compelled to move forward, to seek change. A course such as this is possible when the *first* discovery was not only traumatic but also joyful. This would depend on mother's capacity to mitigate the excitement and to contain it within tolerable levels (this is the purpose of the protective *mist*, of Freud's *Reizschulz*, of Winnicott's "holding," or Bion's "alpha function").

We might call *primal discovery* the first awakening, with the "dream residues" of primary repression. Here, a memory trace of something never perceived and never conscious arises as a perception in consciousness and has to be brought into relation with concurrent perceptions originating from the outside. Freud (1920) found this process startling but he did not elaborate. The uncanny finds its roots here, and so does all creativity. Words we later use, such as fright, amazement, surprise, startle, excitement and joy, but also sadness, echo this moment of an archaic "awesome" discovery. It is this primal discovery that is sought by the second kind of *nostos* – provided its traumatic impact had been within tolerable limits. The wish is not to return to the origins in order to eliminate the insufferable gap of separation but, rather, in order to re-live the excitement of the gap's creation, that confused feeling that what is being discovered is created, the discovery of creation.

Creating something new, as Winnicott among others reminds us, involves the incorporation of the old, of tradition, as when the object as an newly-autonomous entity needs to be linked and integrated with the earlier "subjective object." The process in which the old and familiar is discovered in the new is the basis of creative discovery. This means that the Kleinian depressive position can only be attained and firmly consolidated when its object and the quality of its object relations are aligned and integrated with those of the earlier omnipotent paranoid-schizoid position.

As has been suggested here, the linking of the state of differentiation and the state of fusion generates our sense of time. Our nostalgic Odysseus returns to affirm and to re-affirm his temporality, and, by the same token, his inner contradiction that emanates from that temporality. Recall that Plato saw time as a paradox: He defined it as "the moving image of eternity", associating movement to Number and eternity to immutable Unity (*Timaeus*). Odysseus returns to his past in order to move ahead. Put differently, he returns in order to bring into relation his primal scene (birth) and his final scene (death), scenes which are first telescoped into one, but must be then separated through the intervention of time.

To conclude: A return to the time of primal discovery generates life energy, the energy of Eros, which can then lead to new ventures into the unknown. *Nostos* is, accordingly, a *sine qua non* for new discoveries. There can be no epistemophilic voyage without *nostos*.

Ma misi me per l'alto mare aperto...

Chapter Four

The other journey: *Nekyia*

Stories beget stories. A single word tells a story, and the young child will repeat that word to tell another story which she will find within it and thus learn to speak. Here, I will attempt to tell another story about a story that Odysseus tells in the royal court of Alkinoos, in the course of his *Apologoi* (which form the central part of Homer's story about the Ithakan king).

In Book 10, Odysseus pleads with Kirke to keep her promise and send him home after holding him captive for a year. The "fair-tressed dreadful goddess of human speech" responds to Odysseus' plea with a terrible announcement:

> *Godly son of Laertes, Odysseus of many devices, remain no longer in my house against your will. But, first, it is necessary (χρη, line 490) to complete an other journey (αλλη οδος, line 490) and come to the House of Hades.*

Odysseus must do that, she explains, in order to seek prophecy from the ghost of the blind seer, Teiresias, who will indicate to him the route, the stations and length of his path of return (line 539). Odysseus is stunned by the goddess' words, his spirit is broken and "his heart no longer wished to be alive and behold the light of the sun." Terrified though he is at the prospect of such a voyage to the House of the Dead, his words strangely betray his eagerness to embark on the new venture ("he no longer wished to be alive …").

The question we shall address here is why this journey to the world of the dead is *necessary*. Kirke's explanation is not convincing. As we see in Book 12, she is quite capable of prophesying Odysseus' future herself. To put it differently: Why does the poet, in recounting the manifold adventures of his hero on the surface of the "life-giving earth" and in the open "fish-filled sea", consider it necessary for the completion of his voyage to send him to the underworld, to the world of the shades? What is Odysseus to learn there, this man "who has seen the cities of many men and known the minds of many?"

And so, with a favorable wind, Odysseus and his companions leave Kirke's island behind and sail to the bounds of the earth, to the entrance of the underworld in the land of the Kimmerians (Book 11). Their land is wrapped in mist and cloud. Never does the bright sun shine upon them and deadly night is spread over wretched mortals (lines 15-19). This voyage to the world of the dead, this *alle hodos*, is a night adventure, like a dream, or, perhaps, it *is* a dream. Dreams were believed in Antiquity to be prophetic, and the purpose of this voyage of Odysseus is to have a glimpse of his future. Death (*thanatos*) and

Sleep (*hypnos*) are intimately related in Greek mythology, both being the children of Night (Hesiod, *Theogony*, pp. 76-761). Hermes, the guide of the souls to Hades, holds a golden wand for putting men to sleep or for awakening them (*Odyssey* 24:2-4).

After sailing all day, at sundown Odysseus and his men reach Persephone's grove, the gate to the underworld. Homer (through Kirke's mouth) gives a rather intriguing description of this dark site of the entrance to Death's kingdom, a description of a lush place that might be equally appropriate as a portrayal of the entrance to the primordial womb, to the origin of life:

> *When you reach with your ship the stream of Okeanos, where there is the brush-covered shore and grove of Persephone, with tall poplars and willows that shed their fruit, there beach your ship by the deep-eddying Okeanos and go yourself into the humid house of Hades* (10: 508-512)

What follows are the ritual offers to the dead, first a libation of milk, honey, wine, water, and barley and then a sacrifice of animals which draws the multitudes of shades around the sacrificial pit. The phantoms of the dead, after drinking the sacrificial blood, regain their speech and memory and, by virtue of that, become "alive" again. But Odysseus, with his sword drawn, keeps them all at a distance until he converses with Teiresias. The first ghost that he meets (other than Elpenor who is still unburied and, hence, not yet fully an inhabitant of Hades) is his dead mother, Antikleia. Odysseus, learning that she is dead, weeps at her sight but, despite his deep sorrow, will not let her drink of the blood until he receives guidance from Teiresias. The shade of the blind seer comes next. Among the empty shades he is the only one to whom Persephone has granted a mind (νοος) so that his mental powers remain unimpaired even in the underworld (10: 493-4). He recognizes Odysseus and speaks to him even before drinking of the blood, but he prophesies only after doing so. The blind prophet, now inhabiting the world of the invisible, foresees Odysseus' future: If Odysseus is to see his native land again, it will be after a long and painful journey, after losing all of his comrades, reaching home on a ship that is another's and finding troubles there. He may succeed in his *nostos* if he "chooses to restrain his impulses" (11: 105) during the many adventures that still await him. The linking of blindness with knowledge in the prophet who can see what cannot be seen (i.e., the notion that the future can only be seen with eyes closed), may be an allusion to the prophetic property of dreams, but would also express the (blind) poet's intuition that the future is somehow inscribed in the inner world, that events of the future are shaped by psychic forces. And this is, of course, at a time when no such concept of inner life existed as such.

Then comes a notable passage which, from our perspective, might be the most important part of Teiresias' address to Odysseus. After all, as has already been mentioned, the hardships awaiting him could, and will, soon be made known to him by Kirke. The need, however, for still another journey after reaching Ithaka in order to *make amends* to Poseidon for blinding his son Polyphemos is announced to Odysseus only by the old prophet in the underworld. And, again, as with Elpenor, the story points to an oar, planted on the earth as a memorial, a ship's wings but also a winnowing fan in the final reconciliation of Earth and Ocean: Teiresias' instruction to Odysseus is that after reaching Ithaka he must, taking a shapely oar, travel again far away until he, "whose flesh has been soaked in salty seas", comes to people who know nothing of the sea and eat their food unsalted and who will mistake his oar for a winnowing fan. There he must do honors to the lord of the sea and then depart for home where gentle death will come to him in ripe old age *ex halos* (out of the sea). There is an ambiguity of this last expression, already noted by commentators through the ages: εξ αλος may be understood as meaning death "away from the sea", but also death "at sea." However, the message in Teiresias' words is quite clear: Odysseus will not be able to end his wanderings and find his place on this earth until he makes *reparation* to the injured Poseidon.

The scene that follows is considered, here, central in terms of its psychological impact on the hero and the subsequent evolution of the narrative. It also gives us a glimpse into the Homeric conception of the world of the dead. This is the meeting of Odysseus with the phantom of his dead mother. The scene condenses a number of intensely emotional interactions between mother and son, on a number of interdigitating levels oriented along time and space dimensions. The intensity is tightly "contained" by a mirror-symmetrical arrangement of the dialogue between them which peaks at the end with the son's total bewilderment as he finds himself face-to-face with the void left behind by the absent object. The dialogic symmetry leading up to this existential gap begins with Antikleia inquiring about Odysseus' presence in the world of the dead and ends with Antikleia's answer to Odysseus' inquiry about *her* presence there. In-between there is Odysseus' answer to Antikleia and his questioning her about the circumstances of her death, then about the situation of his father and his son and, finally, about Penelope. Antikleia will answer these in reverse order, ending up with the reasons of her death, which she describes as being "robbed of honey-sweet life" by her longing for him. She emphasizes that it was no illness that took her life but his going away. Her repetition of "you" or "your" (σος, σα, σε: 202-3), clearly points to Odysseus as the cause of her death. Not surprisingly, in the logic of the mythic narrative (as well as in that of the Unconscious) Odysseus' guilt can only be assuaged by re-vitalizing her through giving her blood to drink.

Let us look at this scene in greater detail. Teiresias has just finished his prophesies about Odysseus' return, presumably the reason for which Odysseus had come to the underworld. Yet Odysseus does not show much interest in this, almost dismissing it as the affairs of the gods. His response to what he has been told by Teiresias is in one line: "Teiresias, the gods themselves have woven these things." Instead, he turns his interest away from the future and *towards the past*. His uppermost concern now is his mother, her not looking at him and not speaking to him. He says to Teiresias:

> *But come, tell me and explain exactly: I see here the phantom of my dead mother; she sits in silence near the blood but cannot bring herself to look upon the face of her own son, nor speak to him. Tell me, my lord, how could she recognize me that it is I?*

This corresponds to a moment of overwhelming primitive anxiety in infancy when the infant is mirrored in the face of a dead mother. Recognition or non-recognition is one of the principal themes of the *Odyssey*, but here we see it in its most elemental, its most radical form, as a terrifying unbridgeable gap that separates mother and son. The old prophet explains it with words which, ironically, he characterizes as "easy": The dead will speak and recognize you if you offer them to drink of the sacrificial blood; if you refuse it to them, they will go away. The direction of the feeding and of recognition is reversed here in relation to the situation in infancy. Here, it is not the infant recognizing mother by drinking her milk, but mother herself drinking and recognizing her child; it is not the child "coming alive" through feeding, but mother. None of this, of course, is surprising, as the reference here is to archaic moments prior to me – not-me differentiation. But it is clear that a mutual recognition and a relationship between mother and child is based on orality. And so is punishment and revenge: Antikleia can be starved, has been "starved" and is now thirsty for blood. She drinks and, instantly, recognizes her son.

Odysseus' sudden and dramatic switch of his interest towards the past, the turning of his time orientation back on itself, backwards, is remarkable. All along he has been focused on the future, on the manner of his return home. His descent to Hades was, precisely, in order to consult with Teiresias about his future. But, now, once Teiresias' words are finished, he impatiently turns to the past, to what he has left behind, to his dead mother, to his family in Ithaka and to other personages of his past. This points to Odysseus' *nekyia* (visit to the world of the dead) as an inner descent to the world of memory. The mood throughout this voyage is, as expected, gloomy. The unfolding of time is inseparable from the coming into being of space and *its* unfolding, which creates rupture, loss, and gaps: "Great rivers and frightful streams are between us," says Antikleia, they stand on opposite banks of the river of Death.

Thus, in his temporal switch Odysseus comes face-to-face with loss. The insurmountable gap that separates the future from the past is inhabited by death. Humans perish, according to Alkmaion, because they cannot join the beginning to the end (Kirk and Raven, 1971, Fr. 288, p. 235). The break in continuity cannot be bridged. But it is not the wish to achieve immortality that brings Odysseus to the world of the dead, making him *disthanes* (dying twice). Rather, it is as if he knew that he cannot go forward without first turning back, as if he knew that his future is inscribed in his past and so he returns to it in order to learn the possible avenues of his future. The link, however, between past and future is supplied by death. Thus, Odysseus must descend to the underworld because it is in the encounter with death that past and future can be joined, sutured together through the "now" which is the present, the presence of death. Death, here, functions erotically, as the Great Joiner, the primordial copula. In its pivotal status as the perdurable, actual present death generates time.

The passage from past to future and from future to past is mutative and Odysseus discovers that his nostalgic ($νoστoς$ = return) narcissistic wish to preserve sameness cannot be realized. Continuity can only be achieved at the price of change.

It should be stated, again, that the intention here is not to make a "psychoanalytic study" of the personage of Odysseus through some key scenes in the Odyssean *Nekyia*. Even if such a study were possible, its usefulness would be questionable. Rather, we regard these scenes as universal archetypical situations, as schemas that condense primal formative moments in the development of character. The scene of Odysseus meeting the shadow of his dead mother provides us with such a schema. It could be taken to represent a crucial experience at the earliest stages of psychic growth, at the first encounter with the object, a time when the fundamental question of "present-absent," the very question of Winnicottian "being," makes its first appearance.

At that primal moment, it is mother who "asks" first, so to speak, as she gazes at her newly-arrived child: "My child, how have you come here, below this hazy darkness, yet alive?" In an archaic phantasy, birth and death are at this point commingled, they are yet to be differentiated. The child comes "to be" in a space of, or in a context of, death. It crosses a barrier of which the other side is non-being and mother knows that. In its turn, the child, faced with mother's absence, will raise the same "question" addressed to mother, but inversed: "How did you come to be *not*?" These are the first steps in the foundation of the "primal" object relation, that between mother and infant. It is to the particular manner of negotiating these fundamental issues that the Kleinian concept of a "positions" refers.

The interaction between Odysseus and his mother will soon reach its emotional peak. The son, facing his dead mother (it is now *he* who does not recognize her), bemoans:

> *I wished, thinking anxiously in my mind,*
> *to hold the ghost of my dead mother.*
> *Three times did I rush towards her*
> *as my spirit was driving me to hold her,*
> *and three times did she fly away from my hands*
> *like a shadow or a dream*

Here is depicted that incomprehensible moment when mother is *not*, when the object, solid in its (affective) presence, suddenly disappears into nothing, turns into thin air. The entire course of psychic development can be said to represent ways of dealing with this foundational experience. As an irreducible "fact," it can never be fully accepted, only tolerated in varying degrees. The mirror image of this primordial puzzle, that is how something can come into being from nothing, has been a conundrum haunting philosophers, physicists, as well as the rest of humanity since the emergence of thought.

Mother's "answer" to the child's plea (Odysseus: "Why mother, do you not stay for me, when I wish to hold you?") introduces an inalterable external reality that makes here its first violent appearance: "Oh my poor child ... such is the way of mortals when they die ... their soul, like a dream fluttering off flies away." Absence, loss, void are inexplicable and no answer can ever be "good enough." The child, however, can *dream* and, there, the child can meet the lost object. He/she will later construct symbols and thoughts to bridge the gap. And will speak "flying words" (επεα πτεροεντα) to tell stories.

This scene of Odysseus and Antikleia in the *Odyssey* has its counterpart in the *Iliad*. In Book XXIII, after the death of Patroklos and Achilles' revenge on Hektor, Achilles, mourning, withdraws to "the edge of the fluttering sea where endless waves splash upon the shore." There, exhausted as he was, he is overtaken by "sweet sleep." While asleep, the image of luckless Patroklos appears to him exactly as he was in life, the same stature, the same voice, dressed in the same clothes. Patroklos entreats his friend not to delay his burial so that he can stop wandering and pass through the Gates of Hades and, then, asks Achilles to give him his hand for the last greeting. He predicts Achilles' own demise at Troy's walls, and implores him to make arrangements for their bones to be placed in the same urn. Achilles promises to fulfill all of Patroklos' requests and begs him to come closer so that they can throw their arms around each other and soothe their sorrow:

> *As soon as he [Achilles] spoke thus,*
> *he reached forth with loving hands but he grasped nothing.*
> *The spirit, like smoke, rushed beneath the earth,*
> *with a piercing cry.*

Achilles, startled, wakes up and, despairing, smites his hands together. Here, again, the beloved object that was there a moment ago suddenly and incomprehensibly disappears, vanishing like vapor. The painful moment when the desiring body comes into contact with nothing is dramatized in the Iliadic scene by the gesture of the two hands coming together, clasping nothingness. At this archetypical moment the task of constructing mental representations still lies ahead, as well as that of separating subject and object. The Odyssean scene and its predecessor in the *Iliad* seek to grasp in poetic imagery these primordial moments of psychic development.

These two Homeric scenes that stage in a schematic fashion the earliest articulation of the enigma of presence-absence (death) that will define all of man's subsequent searches also point to the inextricable association of this enigma with the confusing relation between dream and reality. In the Odyssean scene it is in the world of the dead that the hero encounters the shadow of the lost object (i.e., its psyche); in the Iliadic scene, it is in sleep. The mythic equivalence between *thanatos* and *hypnos* – which allows us to speak of an *oneiric nekyia* – has already been pointed out. In the Iliadic dream, psyche is likened to smoke; in the odysseian misty-smoky world of the dead, psyche is likened to a dream. Two centuries later, another poet will proclaim man to be the "dream of a shadow" (Pindar, *Pythia* VIII: 96). The shadow of the absent object is found in the dream. And Herakleitos will muse on life's being death's dream, as death may be a dream of the living.

But returning to Odysseus and his mother, having told him about the destiny of mortals in the dark kingdom of Hades, Antikleia now urges him: "Quickly now, you must desire (λιλαιεο) light." The temptation to remain permanently attached to the lost object, the dead object, is most powerful. For Odysseus, this voyage to the world of the dead is, in a sense, the realization of his *nostos*, a return to his origins. Here, he finds his native soil, so to speak, his mother. Taking leave of her is no easy matter. Persephone's sacred grove is a deadly womb, a return to which can only be fatal. Here, Gorgo's monstrous countenance threatens to freeze him in eternal immobility (11: 634). Quickly, he must feel a desire for light, for life!

But *how* can this come about? Antikleia's last words point the way: "Hold these things in your mind so that you may later speak of them to your wife." The "speaking" here recalls the equivalence of speaking and being alive that we saw earlier when the phantoms of the dead drank of the sacrificial blood. Words are bridges: Speaking constitutes a relation to the object and it could be said that it is object-relating that constitutes "living." Penelope, alive, is to take the place of Antikleia who is the *matrix* of the past, now dead. And Odysseus is to learn to speak to the present object and narrate things "remembered," as a poet-bard does. When he tells the story of his adventures in the court of Alkinoos – the same story that he will later recount to Penelope – Alkinoos praises him that he tells his tale with the skill of a bard. So, the desire that drives man towards life is channeled through words that establish links with objects. These words carry the memory of past objects lost and form bridges with the objects of the present. Speech is fundamentally Erotic.

In this reference of the poet to tales that his hero is to tell when he rejoins the world of the living, there may be an allusion to the poet's mission to be the link, through the word, between present and past, between the living and the dead. Antikleia's instruction to Odysseus that he should keep these things in mind so that he may later speak of them to his wife points to the need for bringing together and *integrating* two worlds, the world of darkness (*zophos*) and the world of light (*phos*), death and life, dream and waking reality. In the course of Odysseus' telling the story of his underworld voyage to the spellbound Phaeakians such an integration is called for as he comes to a stop and turns to practical concerns of everyday present reality, such as the lateness of the hour and the need for sleep. Apart from this representing a technical manoeuvre, part of a bard's strategy, to heighten the dramatic tone of his narrative and to stimulate his audience's interest in the story, it, also, achieves a skillful juxtaposition of the world of the dead with the world of the everyday concerns of the living. When Odysseus returns to the recounting of his experiences in the underworld after Alkinoos' prompting, the reality of the "now," of the living present and its physical time, has been injected, so to speak, into the world of the dead. And, conversely, as the scene at the palace of Scheria is "invaded" by the other world (the world of the dead), the other world is brought out and into the reality of the living. Hence the skillful so-called "intermezzo" of fifty-five lines (lines 330-385) achieves a narrative integration of phantasy and reality, of past and present, which echoes the integration required in the course of psychological development. The cycle of two alternating worlds that need to be integrated is repeated, of course, daily in the sleep-dream/awake/sleep-dream sequence.

The question now, however, is *what* will enable the hero, or the infant, to feel a "desire for the light" and so, to move out of that shadowy world of ill-defined shapes and to come alive.

It is clear that mourning for lost objects, and more specifically for the primary object, is the central theme in the hero's journey to the world of the dead and it is what determines the general mood of the *nekyia*. The loss experienced in the key scene with Antikleia is irreversible. The spatial gap between mother and son ("great rivers are between us ...") is irrevocable. If the self is to differentiate and live as a subject separate and distinct from its original fusional *matrix*, it must mourn and come to tolerate loss through the formation of symbols. The object can then be "re-found," but only after it has been successfully mourned. Through the mourning process the self will be freed and enabled to make a transition to the world of light where it can complete its project – a project, however, that breaks with the past and becomes possible only once the world is *objectified*, rendering the future unpredictable and unknown.

A sense of personal responsibility and guilt, a recognition of one's greed and destructiveness, brings about regret and a need to repair, to make amends. But here a serious problem can arise. The reparation made to the dead and damaged object, whose importance is vital, can be attempted via *concrete* means entailing a sacrifice ("blood for blood"). The re-vitalization of the dead internal primary object is urgent because it is this object, reconstituted as a good and alive internal object, that will provide the core of the self's identity. In the case of Odysseus, it will allow him to no longer be *Outis* (No-one). However, re-vitalization by means of a concrete reparation will not achieve its intended purpose and will require the obsessive repetition of sacrifices, at a great cost to a bleeding and depleted self. Hence, the significance of the *oar* in the story. The damaged or dead objects carried inside the self *must* be given a voice and memory (i.e., they must be re-animated), if the self is to be alive and creative and able to keep alive the hope of reaching its destination, and this can only be achieved by pursuing an *alle hodos*. But the manner of "re-animation" of the dead object is crucial. Thus, in the course of his visit to the world of the dead Odysseus learns that the injured Poseidon will be appeased and will no longer persecute him if he erects a monument and a place of worship to the god ("*there, plant on the earth your well-balanced oar*") in the land of people who do not recognize him. Elpenor's ghost, too, will find peace if Odysseus gives him a burial and raises a monument to the memory of an unlucky man ("*And plant an oar on the mound, the oar that I rowed in life with my comrades*"), otherwise he would become the gods' wrath descending upon Odysseus. This means that the required reparation, in order to be effective and permit growth in the self, must take the form of a σημα (= funerary monument). The planted oar as a *sema* is a symbolic representation of the dead object, its reconstitution *in abstracto*. It is the result of a creative act – and the prototype of all creativity – made possible by the painful process of mourning. The vanished object that leads the exasperated Achilles to strike his hands together in a desperate effort to grasp what is no longer there can be brought back to life again, but *only as a symbol*, charged with semantic value. This is what Orpheus (Virgil, *Georgics* IV; Ovid, *Metamorphoses*) had to learn, alas when it was too late: Euridice could be brought back from the world of the dead but only as a symbol, a thought.

Thus, the primitive phantasy of having depleted the object of its substance through greedy oral demands leading to a compulsive need to feed the dead object with "sacrificial blood" (the result of self-sacrifice) is catastrophic to the self, unless the self succeeds in transforming the concrete compensation to the damaged object into an abstract one through symbolic elaboration. This comes as the result of a most complex developmental process whose outcome remains forever precarious. The process involves the autonomy of phantasy and its derivatives, but this topic cannot be pursued further here.

As for Odysseus, it must be added that if his aim in descending to the underworld was to give voice to the dead and to consult with them, to give them life so that they become a source of inner strength to him, the purpose of his journey was *also* to give them a proper burial and to let them die. Buried beneath a tomb that "speaks," a memorial *sema* that represents them, their existence is to continue from now on as semantic structures. It is towards this end that Antikleia urges on Odysseus with her poignant entreaty: "But now hurry to the light!"

It would appear, therefore, that symbols have a true reparative capacity. Their formation, however, requires the successful outcome of the complex and painful process of separating from the original *matrix*. The process of self-object differentiation occurs in parallel with the differentiation of a thing's representation from the thing, a process that yields true symbols as opposed to "symbolic equations" (Segal, 1957). These developments are parallel and occur simultaneously because the thing is, in fact, a part-object (Klein, 1935) and is attached to, or is part of, the original mother-infant fusional object which undergoes a process of separation and differentiation.

Successful mourning of the loss of the original object allows the co-existence of a subject and an autonomous object, as well as the co-existence of two interacting but distinct worlds, the internal and the external, which can be bridged over by symbols. Symbols, insofar as they are constituted of the integrated co-presence of the object and its absence, can be said to be "whole objects" (Klein, 1935), containing both love and hate parts. Further, as bridges, they restore a particular kind of continuity after the original rupture of differentiation in space and in time has taken place.

Odysseus' descent to the underworld takes him to the abode of the *psychae*. But since the psyche is said to be like a dream (11: 222), Odysseus' voyage is, in fact, a visit to the world of dreams (as alluded to earlier), which he undertakes in order to encounter the life of the psyche. Through Odysseus' presence among them the *psychae* re-connect with their emotions and thoughts that relate them to objects lost and left behind forever and, thereby, become "animated." Their re-activation as objects of the hero's past and their transformation into mental entities constitutes psychic growth. We might say that Odysseus in this underworld journey acquires a psyche in the modern sense, a psyche as a container of memorials to lost objects, some of which are still unburied and lack a tomb (i.e., are not yet properly mourned), while others are mourned and transformed into symbols invested with noetic existence. In the history of ideas, however, it would take a gradual evolution over the three centuries that followed Homer before the precursor of the modern concept of psyche could emerge in the fifth century.

We are now in position to suggest an answer to the question of the reason – of the "*necessity*," we are told in Homer – for the hero's descent to the world of the dead. Odysseus had travelled far on the surface of the earth and in stormy seas and had come to know the minds of many men. But his knowledge would always be incomplete unless he, also, journeyed *beneath* the surface, following the *alle hodos* that would take him to the reality of the *other* world, the concealed domain where psyche resides reminiscing of things lost. It is only by means of such a voyage that he could come to construct an autobiography as a narrative that integrates the reality of *both* worlds. And so, the "dreaded goddess of human speech" directed him to "the other route" that would put him in touch with what can no longer be touched being irretrievably lost, that would place him face-to-face with the non-physicality of the specter, with the incomprehensibility of non-being, so that he could separate from and mourn the loss of objects of his past, and, in addition, through the experience of loss acquire a sense of time.

Restoring dead objects to life so that they can be a source of strength is to be effectuated, not through a sacrifice of the self, but by transforming them into symbols, an essential act of reparation. It could be said that *Homo sapiens* became humanized and truly sapient, not when he started burying his dead, but rather when he started erecting monuments over their grave (*sema*), thereby endowing lost objects with a semantic or symbolic quality.

Thus, we conclude that *Nekyia*, as a part of the hero's adventures in the *Odyssey* or as a process of psychological growth, is a necessary visit to objects lost and un-mourned, or incompletely mourned, in order to complete their mourning and, consequently, free the self to complete its own project. The self's view of reality is enhanced through this process, as the limits of the self (spatial and temporal) are now better defined.

The importance of the "other journey" in constructing a complete autobiographical narrative brings to mind Parmenides' allegorical *proemion* to his Poem *The Way of Truth*. Here, the poet travels not to the Underworld, but through the Gates of Night and Day, guarded by avenging Justice, to the Great Hall of the Goddess, "a place far indeed from the beaten track of men" (the Ucs?). He is welcomed by the Goddess with the following words:

> *I greet you, oh youth...*
> *It is not ill fate that has sent you forth to travel this road*
> *but right and justice.*
> *For it is necessary that you should learn all things,*
> *both the unshakeable core of well-rounded Truth*
> *as well as the common beliefs of mortals*
> (Kirk and Raven, 1971, p. 267).

This voyage, then, through gates that are "bolted with double bolts," brings the traveler in contact with the *well-rounded* truth and allows him to have a complete picture of reality. The goddess' abode in Parmenides' poem is brightly lit, unlike Persephone's dark kingdom in the Epic. But it is clear that Odysseus' underworld journey is not unlike that of the poet-philosopher's in that it is undertaken for the purpose of enhancing his knowledge, of bringing him closer to a *rounded* understanding of himself, an understanding that includes the limitations and the responsibilities of the self.

Descent to the underworld is a theme common to heroic sagas and myths. Thus, Herakles and Theseus, in Greek mythology, go to Hades' dark domain. In Norse mythology, which provided the background to *Beowulf*, the hero plunges to the underwater Hall, in the depths of the haunted mere. But the purpose of such journeys is to accomplish a superhuman feat of extraordinary courage. This is *not* the reason for Odysseus' descent, as it is not the motive for the journey that Gilgamesh, or Aeneas, or Dante undertake. The motive in these cases is a special kind of knowledge, one that cannot be attained otherwise. No heroic act is performed here.

Thus, in the third millennium BCE Sumerian epic *Gilgamesh*, the hero, mourning the loss of his friend and double, goes to the underworld in search of the meaning of life and death. There, he consults with the sage Utnapishtim, the only human to escape the fate of annihilation decreed for all humans. He learns from him that:

> *From the beginning there is no permanence.*
> *The sleeping and the dead, how like brothers they are!*
> (Tablet X, Column vi: 32-33).

We see here the familiar theme of the equivalence between death and sleep, and the reference to the transience of existence, to change and loss. By the way, in Tablet XII, we also have the motif of a hero being *seized* by the underworld, which brings to mind Odysseus' fear at the end of his *Nekyia*.

In Virgil's *Aeneid*, Aeneas sees the ghost of his dead father, Anchises, who enjoins him to travel, with Sibylla's assistance, to Pluto's infernal domain, in order consult with him and learn about his future. Sibylla speaks of Aeneas' desire to cross the Stygian waters twice (cf. Odysseus' *disthanes*) and to view twice the night of Tartarus, and the two of them enter the underworld through a deep cavern, at night. Again, we have the theme of the unburied souls beseeching to be buried ("reparative" burial of Misenus, lines 218-330; of Palinurus, lines 439-512) and the key scene between son and, in this case, father:

> *And there he [Aeneas] tried three times*
> *to throw his arms around his father's neck,*
> *three times the shade untouched slipped through his hands,*
> *weightless as wind and fugitive as dream*
> (Virgil, The Aeneid, Book VI: 939-942)

This is the absence that has to be symbolized before the future can be envisaged as a dream that can be realized. Aeneas' comes to know his future and the founding of the city of Rome by him. Virgil, here, collapses the figures of Teiresias and Antikleia into one, that of Anchises. As in the earlier epic, the descent is necessary for the subsequent evolution of the narrative. Note, again, the suggested equivalence of the descent to a dream: While Aeneas and Sibylla enter the underworld through the mouth of a cavern, they exit through Sleep's Ivory Gate, the gate of deceptive dreams (cf. *Odyssey* 19: 562-567).

But let us return to the Homeric *Nekyia*, to the hidden world where psyches reside, and ask what Odysseus might have learned during what we would consider as his inner journey.

Odysseus' conversation with his mother has now come to an end: "And we were exchanging such words with each other while the women came, for august Persephone sent them ..." Feminine presence is, unquestionably, a dominant aspect in the *Nekyia*: Odysseus comes to the underground kingdom of Queen Persephone at the behest of the sorceress Kirke, where he meets Teiresias (who has been both a man and a woman), his mother, and now a whole parade of other women flocking around the dark blood, women who were once the wives and daughters of noble men. At the end, Odysseus will leave in a hurry fearing the sight of Gorgo's monstrous head. With all this emphasis on women, it is not surprising that, when he stops his account in the Phaeakian court due to the lateness of the hour, it is the Queen who breaks the silence of the entranced audience with words of praise for a man of "balanced mind."

The king, however, wishes to hear more and, specifically, of the fate of the godlike heroes who undertook the expedition to Troy. Extolling Odysseus' bardic skills, he convinces him to continue his story. Only now does Odysseus speak of the ghosts of Agamemnon, of Achilles, and of Aias, finishing, again, with a list of heroes and sinners.

In his meeting the ghost of Agamemnon, we hear of the same sad gesture that Odysseus had made to embrace his mother. The murdered king, shedding bitter tears, stretches his arms to embrace Odysseus but his limbs have now lost the vigor they once had (11: 391-394).

Later, Odysseus meets Achilles. He exalts the hero for being blessed, both in life, being honored equally to gods, and in death, being the mighty leader of the dead. But the ghost of Achilles retorts that he would much prefer to toil in life as the servant of a poor farmer than be the lord of the dead. This must, surely, impress Odysseus who has known Achilles to value a short but glorious life more than a long, contented but insignificant one, and to place, unlike Odysseus himself, *kleos* above *nostos*. In Achilles' humble plea for an ordinary life we see a radical re-definition of heroic values of valor and martial glory as we hear of them in the *Iliad*.

Then comes Odysseus' striking encounter with Aias, accompanied by an unprecedented monologue. The throng of ghosts crowds around Odysseus, but one alone stands aloof keeping his distance: Aias, still in rage for Odysseus' victory in the contest over Achilles' arms. Odysseus the narrator, deeply troubled, addresses his Phaeakian audience, still struggling with his guilt:

> *I wish I hadn't won in such a contest*
> *for, on account of those arms, the earth claimed such a head,*
> *Aias, who, in build and deeds of war, stood among all the Danaans*
> *next to the illustrious son of Peleus* (548-552).

In the underworld, Odysseus speaks to Aias saying:

> *Aias, son of noble Telamon, were you not, then,*
> *even in death, to forget your wrath against me*
> *on account of those accursed arms?* (553-555).

He praises him as the tower of the Argives, for whom "we" grieved as much as for the loss of Achilles, and ends by pleading with him:

> *But come closer, my lord, and listen to my words and to my story*
> *and tame your anger and proud spirit.*

Aias, however, unmoved, walks away without speaking a word.

This is a remarkably changed Odysseus who speaks these words, obviously sincerely touched. There seems to be something in *him* that has been tamed. His pride subdued, he regrets his victory over Aias that led to the latter's humiliation and suicide. Teiresias' prophecy and counsel to make amends to Poseidon, his mother's empty shadow and her poignant words, Achilles' sad yearning for a humble life must all have had a profound impact on him. The compassionate attitude that we see in his encounter with Aias cannot but be related, in our listening to the story, and certainly somewhere in the poet's mind, to the various emotionally charged experiences that he has had in the course of his visit to the underworld.

So, what has Odysseus learned in the course of that journey? He has learned that his mother is dead and that this means that she can now only exist as a dream, as an image in his mind; that her physical body will be forever elusive to him despite his sorrow and yearning to be united with her again. He has learned that regret and the wish to compensate for injuries inflicted are wise but can only come with old age. He has learned the importance of restrain, and that human lives are not exclusively determined by Fate and external powers, human choice playing a pivotal role. He has learned that life at its most humble moments is worth living and should not be sacrificed for narcissistic glory. He has learned that anger must not be endless, and that forgiving and reparation are human and noble. He has learned that the dark, sad world of objects lost and the endless unyielding search for them must be left behind, as life with its dangers, challenges, hopes, and uncertainties surges forward in defiance of the past. And he has learned that the future is linked to the past through the present (the presence of death), a paradoxical link that dis-connects the two and sets them apart thereby freeing the future and creating time as a *spiral* evolution, neither circular, nor linear. And he has learned much more. The self, going through the psychological process of mourning, emerges much strengthened.

In the episodes that follow the *Nekyia*, namely, the encounter of the Sirens and the events in the island with Helios' cattle, we see the impact of these underworld experiences on Odysseus. He resists the regressive deadly lure of the Sirens and, in Thrinakia, he is able to control his instinctual needs (his hunger), unlike his companions who slaughtered and ate the sacred cattle. On the whole, there seems to be a certain shift in the nature of the threats and the dangers that Odysseus recounts that he met before his *Nekyia* and those following it. A ruthless persecutory element appears predominant in the adventures preceding his journey to the underworld, whereas caring, loving, supporting experiences make their appearance and constitute a distinct presence in Odysseus' travels after the *Nekyia* (Kirke's helpful directions, Kalypso's love, and the Phaeakians' hospitality). The projective mechanisms and paranoid anxieties of the earlier adventures now co-exist with depressive anxieties and the introjection of good, loving objects.

The *Nekyia* appears, therefore, to be a turning point. In the carefully designed architectural structure of the poem (Most, 1999), the *Nekyia* is placed at the exact center of the *Apologoi*, with six adventures preceding it and six following it. It is, by far, the longest of the *Apologoi*, occupying an entire Book. All this would seem to justify Finley's (1978) claim that "The Underworld is the apex of the travels" (p. 129), a view echoed by de Jong (2001), who affirms: "The *Nekuia* occupies a pivotal place, both in the *Apologue* and in the *Odyssey*" (p. 271). The centrality of Book 11 is also stressed by Heubeck and Hoekstra (1989), who point to the prominent place it occupies in the poem and to the various ways it affects the subsequent narrative as a pre-condition for Odysseus' *nostos*. Underlining the "internal unity of the story," these authors conclude that "the poet has succeeded admirably in combining motifs from religious practice, folk-tale and saga, and subordinating each to the overall concept of the poem" (pp. 76-77). All this testimony runs counter to claims made by the "analytic" camp of the Homeric Question according to which the *Nekyia* is an amalgamation of stories from different times and is not an integral part of the *Odyssey*. Page (1966), for example, considers the *Nekyia* to have been composed independently by another poet and to have been inserted into the *Odyssey* with some clumsy attempts at integration. Wilamowitz-Möllendorf (1927), also, believes Book 11 to be an interpolation. The approach adopted here adds support to the view that the *Nekyia* is an integral, well-integrated, and essential episode in the *Odyssey*, an episode that is indispensable to the psychological coherence and cohesion of the whole narrative.

The differences in the ideological and psychological climate that distinguish and set apart the two Homeric Epics have been repeatedly noted. Linguistic and philological evidence supports the view that the *Odyssey* was composed a few decades after the *Iliad*. Whether the differences noted reflect social changes that took place in the latter part of the eighth century BCE, shifts in the ideological climate, changes in the aging poet himself, or even different authorship of the two Epics, is not germane to our argument here. What concerns us is the extent to which this change can be considered as an indication of a psychological evolution that occurs as part of the process of maturation. The *Nekyia* would seem to be at the very center of the significant change in climate that we observe as we pass from the *Iliad* to the *Odyssey*. The nature and direction of the mutation that occurs stand out more clearly here in the Eleventh Book of the *Odyssey*. There is a transformation of values that characterize the hero, reflected both in Achilles' words and in the scene of Odysseus with Aias. When Odysseus meets Aias, unchanged and unreachable in his silence, it becomes clear from Odysseus' own words and attitude that something of the old epical values of uncompromising heroism, personal glory, pride, and military honor has changed. We have glimpses of a new *Selbstanschauung*, new dilemmas, and an emerging sense of inner conflict that will, later, be developed by the lyric poets and will, eventually, culminate in the sense of the tragic as we see it in the fifth century. As an example, contrast what Odysseus says to Eurykleia who rejoices at the sight of the dead suitors, with Achilles' exaltation over Hektor's dead body in the *Iliad*. Odysseus restrains (κατερυκε) Eurykleia, saying "Old woman, rejoice in your spirit but hold back and do not shout out in triumph. It is not right to boast over slain men" (22: 411-412), while Achilles, victorious, exclaims: "Come, sons of Achaeans, singing a song of triumph, let us go to the curved ships ... We have won ourselves great renown" (XXII: 391-393).

The different orientation of the two Epics is evident, of course, in the opening lines of each, in the invocation to the Muse. In the *Iliad*, the Muse is enjoined to sing the *wrath* of Achilles that sent so many valiant souls to Hades. In the *Odyssey*, the Muse is called forth to sing the *man* who came to know the minds of many and suffered woes struggling to save his life and that of his comrades. The very first word in the *Iliad* is "Wrath," whereas in the *Odyssey* it is "Man." The hero's descent to the world of the dead in the later epic is no longer a praiseworthy means of achieving manly honor and *kleos*, but a necessary step in the search for knowledge, in a man's struggle to stay alive and return to the warmth of his home and family. There is a kind of down-to-earth humanism in the *Odyssey* which contrasts with the Olympian heroism of the *Iliad*. Fränkel (1986) speaks of a "new humanity" which asserts itself in the *Odyssey*, and of a new kind of heroism that expresses itself in the strength with which the hero masters his feelings (p. 165). Imperceptibly, we are moving towards a new era where the individual is endowed with more responsibility in managing his *moira* and in shaping his inner and outer world. This is clearly not the dominant view in the *Odyssey*, but we see here the seeds of what is to develop over the next three centuries. The particular form of Teiresias' prophecy testifies to that new orientation: "If you *choose* to hold back your impulses ... you may reach home." The idea is new and, surely, the poet is as uncertain and uncomfortable about it as is his hero, who rushes to affirm: "Teiresias, of all these things, the gods themselves must have spun the thread." Odysseus seems to find the burden of being responsible for his own actions overwhelming, and tries to evade it (as he does, in a similar way, at a moment of painful guilt when faced with Aias, in 558-560). There is another instance in the *Odyssey* where it is suggested that it is not only gods who determine the actions of humans. In Book 4, the herald Medon, answering Penelope's anxious questions about the whereabouts of her son Telemachos, says: "I do not know whether it was some god who moved him, or whether he was driven by his own impulse to go to Pylos" (4: 712-714).

The introduction of personal choice in the management of human affairs brings into play opposing forces within the now autonomous individual, leading to ambivalence, inner conflict, and the need for restraint and self-control. A line such as Sappho's "*There is something I yearn to tell you, but shame holds me back*" could only have been written in late seventh century. Jacqueline de Romilly (1991) points to the earliest expression of inner division and conflict in the Ancient World, which she finds in the *Odyssey* (20: 18): Odysseus murmurs to himself at a moment of rage "*Hold back my heart!*" The movement that will eventually lead to the appearance of tragedy in the fifth century begins here.

It would seem that the entire course of human psychological development is aimed at the attainment – or approximation – of what might be called the "tragic position." Would that be, also, the aim of the "descent to the other world" by following the *alle hodos* and, indeed, the aim of psychoanalysis?

Chapter Five

The tragic in the *Iliad*

The appearance of attic tragedy in the fifth century BCE was the result of a complex process initiated by the convergence of a number of social, political and psychological factors that expressed shifting ideologies. A gradual and lengthy transformation of existing social organizational patterns and religious beliefs led to a radical redefinition of the individual's place in society and his perception of reality, both internal and shared. Once it made its appearance as a new art form, tragedy played a major role in shaping human consciousness, at least Western consciousness, and forever changed our vision of reality. The process was circular in that, as tragedy came to articulate, elaborate, and work-through deeply rooted human concerns and anxieties related to new emerging situations, it shaped, in turn, our view of these phenomena. Tragedy is a mirror of its roots.

The dimension that is of particular interest to us in the developments that led to attic tragedy is the psychological one and the factor that we consider to have been a primary determinant of that process is the emergence and evolution of the concept of *psyche* (ψυχη). For Homer, psyche was the principle of life (ψυχειν = to breathe). It was believed to continue its existence after death in the form of a shadow, an *eidolon*. Rohde (1893) in the 19th century attributed the emergence of the concept of the psyche in Antiquity to the experience of seeing the dead in dreams (cf. Achilles dreaming of the dead Patroklos in *Iliad* XIII: 65), as well as to experiences of religious ritual trance. Pythagorean beliefs were soon grafted onto the Homeric concept to give rise to the notion of an immortal psyche. It must be stressed, however, that the predominant view in Homeric times was that the seat of human action is in the will of the Olympians. Nevertheless, there are instances in the Epics where a decision to act in a particular way is the result of an inner dialogue in the mind of the hero himself. A notable example of this is towards the end of the *Iliad* (XXII: 98-130). Here, Hektor facing Achilles for what is to be his final battle and demise "speaks to his spirit" deliberating on what his best course of action should be. Should he go ahead and fight winning victory or perishing, or should he lay down his shield and come to an agreement with Achilles yielding to the Achaeans by returning Helen and promising them half of the city's treasures? In agonizing over what decision to take, he suddenly stops and asks: "But why is my mind debating these things?" The verb used by Homer is διαλεξατο, to "carry on a dialogue" with himself about what to do. He decides to fight.

In the three centuries that followed there were significant developments in the concept of psyche introduced by the lyric poets (e.g.,

Archilochos, Sappho) and by the pre-Socratic philosophers (notably, Herakleitos). Psyche was now believed to be the seat of thought, desire and will. This "psychological" psyche gradually merged with the immortal psyche, and this eventually gave rise to the Platonic concept of a composite psyche.

The major shift that these developments entailed was that the seat of human action was now gradually moving down from Olympus to the depths of the individual human soul. The old gods were beginning to recede, as a new anthropocentric universe – what we came to call "humanism" – was emerging. This was a movement from *mythos* to *logos*.

But humanism comes with a price. Plato's *psyche* is composite: it contains three parts ("appetitive," "thymic" and "rational") and these cannot but enter into *conflict* with each other (the similarity to Freud's concept of the psyche cannot be missed – the "thymic" coming close to the superego). Conflict fragments human experience, thought, feeling, and action. The confrontation from now on will no longer be between human and god, but between human and human. Or, between the wishes of the individual psyche and the laws of the collectivity (of the newly arisen *polis*). Hence *Antigone*'s insurmountable dilemma: two courses of action, both equally justifiable and both equally indefensible. Reality, truth, is irreparably split in two. Reality has multiple faces, and in that Dionysos can claim to rise triumphantly over Apollo (unifying reason). The tragic in human affairs has made its irreversible appearance and a new art form is born to express it.

Tragedy has changed over the past two-and-half millennia as it mirrors evolving social and psychological realities but, insofar as the individual human being continues to be inwardly divided and faced with irresolvable dilemmas between conflicting realities and the incomprehensibility of death, the genre of tragedy cannot disappear. There is unquestionably a profound affinity that links Aeschylus and Sophokles with Ibsen and Beckett.

In the present chapter we shall look for the tragic before the appearance of tragedy as a specific art form. We shall explore its earliest manifestation in Western literature, in the *Iliad*. An attempt to give it a definition will be based on the examination of the generally accepted aspects of the theory of the origins of tragedy, a theory that originated with Aristotle.

THE TRAGIC

Aristotle's influential theory of the origins of tragedy was based on the earlier testimony of Herodotos (*Historiae* 5: 67). In his treatise on poetry, Aristotle (1995) held that the origins of tragedy can be traced back to the dionysian satyr chorus and associated dithyramb hymns. A rich scholarship on the topic followed over the succeeding centuries involving philosophers, historians, philologists, and anthropologists. As a result of all this, and despite passionate disagreements on specifics, few would doubt today the existence of an evolutionary link between tragedy and the earlier satyr choruses and associated dithyramb hymns in honor of Dionysos.

The presence of Dionysos on Greek soil is now attested to date from the Bronze Age. Excavations at Aghia Eirene in Kea have brought to light a fifteenth century BCE sanctuary of Dionysos, and evidence from Linear B tablets from Pylos suggest that worship of Dionysos was already established in Mycenean times. Although tragedy gradually grew away from its early beginnings in dionysian ritual and progressively "acquired its own nature" (*Poetics* 1449a15), its link to Dionysos remained evident in its direct association with the god's festivals during the classical period.

If it is generally accepted that there is a close connection between tragedy and the worship of Dionysos, we might gain some useful insights on the nature of the tragic by examining that elusive figure of the "mad god," as Homer calls him (*Iliad* VI: 132).The first characteristic of the god that we come upon, however, is precisely his resistance to a fixed identity. He is the god of the Several, of multiple realities, of fluid transformations, and of the dissonant co-existence of contradictory states. When Pentheus, in Euripides' *Bacchae* (Kirk, 1970), asks who this god is, the answer he receives is "Whosoever he wishes to be!" (*Bacchae*, line 477). Dionysos' multiple identities nevertheless contain a common theme encountered in myths related to him. This is the theme of violent dismemberment (*sparagmos*), of fragmentation, so powerfully depicted by the old Euripides in his *Bacchae*. Dionysos was known as *anthroporraistes*, "he-who-tears-humans-apart." He himself, as a child, was torn to pieces by the Titans at the command of Hera, the Mother Goddess. Mothers who follow him (Leukippe, Procne, the women of Argos, the Proitidae, and others) tear their children apart as they are seized by dionysian frenzy. It seems that the god's very identity is fragmented, variable or dispersed, made of multiple opposing parts. A god of two births (by Semele and by Zeus), Dionysos is both divine and animal, both young and old, both man and woman. Fundamentally, he is the god of contradictory dualities, *Di*-onysos of the *di*–thyrambos, of the "tragic dissonance" (Nietzsche, 1954) of human nature.

As the god of wine, merriment and orgiastic revelry, allowing humans to escape the hardships and sorrows of daily life, he is, in Homer's words, the "joy of mortals" (XIV: 325). But his influence goes beyond states of wine intoxication. His frenzied followers enter a state of divine ek-stasy (*enthousiasmos*), abandoning their ordinary everyday identity to become one with the god. He is the god of altered states of being, of altered identities, of sanity and of madness. Hence his mask, as an embodiment of that duality of being.

A more dreadful transformation, however, is concealed behind the mask. The joy of mortals, the vegetation god of fertility, of ivy staves (as we see him in the *Bacchae*), of young maidens nursing forest beasts, of idyllic innocence and serene rapture, a god "most gentle" to wretched humans, suddenly appears in his other frightful countenance as the chthonic ruthless sovereign of the darkest forces of savagery, a "most dreadful god" (*Bacchae*, line 861). The other side of his mask reveals him to be the Lord of the Souls, the son of the Queen of the dead, Persephone. Walter Otto (1981) points out that many dionysian festivals (Anthesteria, Agrionia) were in honor of the dead, and underlines the intrinsic mutuality between the cult of birth and the cult of the dead. Otto points out that, after descending to the innermost core of existence, which is inhabited by the forces of life, one re-emerges with a look of madness because, in that netherworld, life co-habits with death (*Dionysus, Mythus und Kultus*, 1933). Burkert (1983), on the other hand, shows that the link between wine and blood is ancient. Ikarios, to whom Dionysos revealed the art of making wine, was slain by other peasants and his daughter hanged herself.

Thus, in the end, the god of the fragmentary character of human experience is the god of the primeval duality of Life and Death, of Eros and Thanatos. His mask is a mask of death. Herakleitos, the "obscure," lucidly asserts, at the end of a fragment that contains a masterful *jeu de mots*: "Hades and Dionysos are one and the same" (in the fragment, *aidoion*, the sexual organ related to life, is linked to *aides,* the kingdom of death).

Dionysos' link to the world of the dead lends support to William Ridgeway's (1966) theory that tragedy arose from laments at the tomb of the dead hero. Ridgeway believed that the earliest dithyrambs were composed to be sung around the graves of the mighty dead, and pointed to the fact that tomb ritual lamentations abound in the fully formed tragedies. Although this theory has been challenged, I believe it retains its relevance.

Thus we conclude that the god of tragedy stands for the bewildering fragmentation of human experience, for multiple identity states that slide easily and unpredictably into each other, and ultimately, for the most radical fragmentation of all, that between being alive and being dead.

And so, by looking at the forbidding countenance of the masked god of tragedy, we capture an image of the tragic. The tragic is the fragmentary character of reality, the co-existence of multiple contradictory realities, the reality of death as a fragment of life and of life as a fragment of death. All this is incomprehensible to humans and the source of a perpetual existential Angst which is at the root of all artistic production and philosophical reflection.

Psychoanalysis provides us with a certain perspective as to the origins of this fundamental, indeed foundational raw fact of human experience, namely, the sense of fragmentation. It traces it to the earliest moments of life, to the time even before there is a sense of time in the developing *infans*. This is a primeval, mythical time preceding differentiation, when the world, or being, is lived as being One, an indivisible primal unity of a fusional All. This primal Oneness may be considered as an innate primal phantasy, a psychic "predisposition" genetically encoded, ready to be structured and to structure the individual's experience following birth. It certainly finds support in the experience of the biological state of a fusional oneness of mother-embryo, prior to the separation at birth. But then comes the Big Bang and the sphere splinters. Plato (1973), in the *Symposion*, has Aristophanes recount the myth of the origin of humans which explains "human nature and its suffering" (189d 5-6). At the beginning of our existence, he tells us, we were all creatures of quite a different kind: We were *androgyna*, that is, round, globular, bisexual beings with two faces, four arms, and four legs. These creatures, the Platonic Aristophanes continues, were whole and complete unto themselves, and in time became arrogant and, wanting to be masters of Heaven, challenged the gods. Upon that, Zeus with a swift blow split them in two, in the manner of cutting an apple right down the middle. Anticipating that they would be prone to forget their new status of being only incomplete parts of a Whole, Zeus instructed Apollo to turn the face of each half around toward the gash, so that looking at the wound would make them humble and reasonable. And so, Aristophanes concludes, we came to be what we are today, "a symbol of a human being" (191d 4), divided in two like the fragments of a *symbolon*, forever face-to-face with the wound that defines us and seeking to heal our fragmentary nature and re-constitute our original wholeness.

Human nature is, thus, defined by fragmentation, which is at the root of the process of differentiation. Corresponding to the biological differentiation at birth (two bodies emerging from one), psychoanalysis posits a similar process leading to the birth of the "I", the individual psychic self, differentiated from the "not-I", the Other, and emerging from an original fused psychic Oneness (Winnicott, 1971). This psychological separation comes about as the result of a delicate, complex, and painful process involving mother and infant, a process that is never fully accomplished in an irreversible manner. The experience – in phantasy or in reality – of fragmentation remains throughout the life of the individual as a never completely healed wound that causes pain, profound suffering and disillusionment. Zeus succeeded: The awareness of the unbridgeable gap that separates the race of humans from that of gods – whole and blissful in their perfection and unbroken by death – can only momentarily be forgotten or pushed aside. Repeated attempts to bridge it only intensify our permanent awareness of that puzzling, incomprehensible rift.

The adult's phantasy of an original narcissistic state of completeness and of supreme omnipotence that was subsequently lost through a violent scission that resulted in differentiation implicates mother as the agent responsible for the tragic rupture. It is here that the act of birth becomes, in phantasy, intrinsically bound and experientially identified, on the deepest level, with a murderous act. Mother, according to the (unconscious) phantasy, murders her infant at the moment of birth, giving it birth and death at the same time. This explains the dual identity of Dionysos as the god of fertility and of death. It also explains the constant theme of mothers murdering, dismembering, and devouring their children in the various versions of the Dionysos myth, culminating in Euripides' horrific dramatization of Agave screaming triumphantly and tearing her son apart at a moment of orgasmic, we might say, ecstasy. His body now lies in pieces ($\chi\omega\rho\iota\varsigma$, 1137), says Euripides, most difficult to find and to bring together: $ov\ \rho\alpha\delta\iota ov\ \zeta\eta\tau\eta\mu\alpha$. This is a poignant portrayal of the never-ending struggle of the individual to bring together and to harmonize deformed, disparate fragments of her existence which are scattered along time and space.

The complex and delicate process of cleavage of the original mother-infant fusional Oneness results in a number of fundamental differentiations that define the psychic life of humans. It is a particular characteristic of these differentiations that the entities set apart are, nevertheless, intimately linked due to their common origin. The negotiation, so to speak, of the nature and *quality* of that link, so that it permits and fosters exchange and emotional closeness between the two opposing sides while affirming their separateness (and resisting regressive fusion), is a major developmental task in the psychological growth of the individual. To the extent that the task is met, the sense of fragmentation is "contained," but it never disappears.

The first psychic differentiation, on which those that follow are based, is the "I" - "not-I" separation. This evolves into an "I" - "Other I" distinction where the Other, although other and different (i.e., a true object), is recognized as bearing an intimate identificatory affinity to the self. This subject - object differentiation unavoidably leads to the categorical duality "present - absent," following experiences where the now autonomous object is absent. The splitting of the object into "good" and "bad" is related to this polarity. From the distinction subject - object also emerges a sense of time as well as a sense of space (see Ch. 3). It is here that the concept of death appears, together with the polarity "living - dead", based on the sense of time and of absence. Further, insofar as the absent object may remain present in thought, a distinction between phantasy and reality will have to come about, and this will eventually progress, as symbols are generated, to the distinction between the thing itself and its symbol.

As we can see, the fragmentation underlying these differentiations takes two basic forms: a) fragmentation of the subject ("I" – "not-I") and b) fragmentation of the object (present - absent, alive - dead).

The enduring presence of the phantasy of a primordial One that splintered at the origin of time to create the various categories of human consciousness maintains the painful sense of the tragic fragmentation of being and of the multiform nature of reality that includes the reality of non-being. The tragic is eventually elevated to a metaphysical principle, considered as a "primary component of the universe" (Scheler, 1972).

THE TRAGIC IN THE *ILIAD*

As the garden poppy bends its head, weighed down by its seeds and the showers of spring, so did he droop his head heavy with his helmet (VIII: 306-8).

In this magnificent metaphor we become witnesses of the fracture of being at the moment it encounters the irreconcilable gap between the bright red of life, of spring, sprouting seeds, promise of future life, and the violent fall of rain, the deadly weight of the suddenly black seed now pulling it to the ground, to its grave. The *Iliad* abounds with such exquisite and exquisitely painful scenes.

It hardly needs to be stressed that the *Iliad*, a poem about the War of Troy, a poem of countless battle scenes of unthinkable atrocity, is, nevertheless, *not* a poem about war, not a poem about fighting. Walter Marg (1973) called it "a poem of death," but it is better characterized as a poem of life and death (Griffin, 1980), as each acquires its meaning in relation to the other. The *Iliad* is, specifically, about how man meets the inevitability of his end, the physical boundaries of his existence. *Moira* is a spatial concept etymologically referring to one's lot, to limits beyond which the individual cannot venture. Perhaps what makes this concept difficult to accept, tolerate, or comprehend is the human evolutionary capacity to be *in thought* outside these boundaries. This is the territory ascribed to the divine. But what this means, in the end, is that the human being becomes the carrier of a contradiction. She can both be and not be outside her limits. She is both constrained within her allotted territory and free to transcend it. The *Iliad* is about transitions and the transcendence of individual boundaries.

The Scholiast (Eustathius), looking at the opening lines that speak of the wrath that sent many valiant souls to Hades, remarks that the Poet "has devised a tragic prologue to his tragedies." He considers the *Iliad* as a unified group of tragedies. With this in mind and based on our definition of the tragic as the fragmentation of human reality into opposing and conflicting parts, let us look, first, at three scenes, taken at random, which illustrate Homer's mastery in portraying tragic dissonance.

A. In Book XXII, Hektor has been slain by Achilles who is now dragging him, stripped of his armor, behind his chariot. Hekabe and Priam witness this and break out in inconsolable lament. Andromache, however, inside the palace, knows nothing about it and is weaving a purple robe, embroidering flowers of many colors on its double folds. She calls her handmaids instructing them to set a great tripod on the fire for Hektor's hot bath when he returns from battle. And the Poet adds in a personal tone: "Poor woman! She could in no way imagine how very far from a bath he lay," struck down as he was by bright-eyed Athena through Achilles' hands. This is tragic irony at its peak. Naked Hektor dead, dragged in mud versus colorful flowers on the folds of a graceful purple bathrobe; a hot bath for the hero returning home (νοστησαντι) versus a funeral bath for the fallen hero. And Andromache, unable to "conceive" (ουδ' ενοησεν) the reality of the situation and the unbridgeable gap that separates her world from the outside. Two parallel, antithetical, mutually exclusive universes and the lone helpless individual torn between them.

B. In Book XII, at the very beginning, there is a remarkable prolepsis. Hordes of men, Argives and Trojans, are hard at battle with each other. But the broad wall that the Greeks built to protect their ships was not to last for long. When the bravest of the Trojans and many of the Argives had died, we are told, and the city of Priam had fallen in the tenth year and the Greeks had returned to their dear native land, then the gods swept away the wall, thrusting against it the fury of rivers descending from the Idaean mountains, the rivers into which "many ox-hide shields, horned helmets and a race of men half-divine had fallen, deep in their silt." The Shaker of the Earth, himself, took the lead and swept up in his waves "all the foundations of beams and stones that the Achaeans laid with so much toil, and he made everything smooth along the strong stream of the Hellespont and covered again the great beach with sand." And "the beautifully-flowing stream flowed as before."

The transience and insignificance of man's conflicts and efforts, nature's indifference, indeed cruelty, its supreme Law of a universal harmony and beauty affirming itself not against man's destruction, but because of it, all of this conveyed through the dramatic juxtaposition in the narration of four moments in time dynamically interacting with each other in a ceaseless back-and-forth. There is the time when men are fighting; the time when they are gone; the time when the land and the rivers return to what they were before; the time of the narration. These fragments of time are made to co-exist in the narrative process so that present, past, and future are interchangeable and depend on one's relative position (e.g., the future is past, the past is future, etc.). In this whirl of time, the word ημιθεοι (demigods) appears as the only instance that Homer uses this epithet. Men whirling around in the orbit of time, whirling around between the world of humans and that of the immortal gods.

C. In Book XXII, the Trojans have been routed and have taken cover inside the City Walls, but Hektor has remained steadfast in front of the City at the Skaean Gates. Old Priam, anticipating his son's fate, implores him to come inside, but is unable to persuade him. It is now Hekabe's turn. Shedding bitter tears she loosens her bosom robe and holds out her breast: "Hektor, my child, for *this* show respect and have pity on me. Remember, if I ever gave you this breast to forget your pain" (λαθικηδεα μαζον). Come inside "my beloved budding shoot that I myself brought to birth." Beseeching him, but to no avail.

At the Gates of death, a disconsolate mother is desperately trying to *reverse* time in order to avert her son's impending death. She invokes the time of his birth and of her breastfeeding him, the budding time of his childhood, abruptly juxtaposed this to his death, now, that stands in front of him. She wants to take him inside again, inside *her*, to protect him. The dismal contrast between "then" and "now" is redoubled in the opposition between the sweet milk flowing out of her, then, and the tears that flow from her now. It is sharpened by her plea to remember his forgetting life's pain while falling asleep at the breast then, now that he is about to be enshrouded by the sleep of death. She is struggling to neutralize Thanatos infusing it with Eros, but the two cannot be brought together because the gulf of time keeps them apart. Again, two discordant realities side by side and humans caught between them.

The contrasting co-existence of opposing irreconcilable realities is the background against which – and in relation to which – all action takes place in the *Iliad*. It is the sharply defined dominant perspective that bestows meaning to each event. The central regulatory principle of that perspective is the notion of *time*. It is the dimension which is at the root of all the disorganizing gaps of human experience. These are the gaps that the individual experiences in the living out of disparate and contradictory states, at the core of which is his confrontation with death. Fragmentation is felt by the individual in his assuming different states of being, along islands of space and of time. Before proceeding to give examples of this, however, a few words should be said about time at the time of Homer.

R. B. Onians (1989) correctly points out that Homer's time is not homogeneous but, rather, a quality attached to different experiences at different moments or situations in the life of an individual. This underlines the fragmented nature of the sense of time in Homer which is the basis of the discontinuity and unpredictability of human experience. Alkmaion's dictum that humans perish because of their inability to join their end to their beginning reflects the Homeric view of discontinuous time. Various experiences in the life of the individual, but also in the life of different individuals, occupy their own segment of time – or, better, the segment of time allotted to them. The poignant image in Book VI of the generations of men springing up and passing away like the generation of leaves scattered by the autumn wind and then burgeoning forth anew finds its echo in Alkmaion's statement and stresses the disconnected character of existence. The thread of time may be sequential but is fragmented.

In the course of the three or four centuries that followed Homer the notion of time evolved towards a concept of a homogeneous, continuous, and uninterrupted order of nature. Under Orphic and Pythagorean influence, time became circular, the time of eternal returns and of the harmonious movement of the celestial spheres. For Plato, it was the "moving image of eternity" (*Timaeus*). This new conception of time led to the principle of Eternal Truths that exist unaffected by time and in opposition to the perpetual change of material things. The emphasis in the Classical period is on permanence. Even recollection ($αναμνησις$) is, for Plato, not a reflection on the past and on change, but, rather, a means of accessing what is changeless and timeless (see Vernant, 1996). This is not the case, however, in the Epics which emphasize metaphysical transience and irreversible change. This may be another way of understanding Plato's intolerance of Homer.

Some selected examples of the sense of fragmentation of human experience, as we hear them presented in the *Iliad*, will now follow. They correspond, on the whole, to the rifts created in the course of psychic differentiation that were mentioned above: I—You, Living—Dead, Reality—Phantasy.

We begin with *temporal* segments of contrasting contradictory existential states. The general theme, here, is expressed by Apollo in Book XXI: You would consider me mad, he tells Poseidon, if I were to fight with you on account of wretched mortals who

> *are like leaves: at one time*
> *full of life's fire ...*
> *and at another, wasting away lifeless.*

Earlier in the same Book, we have the moving scene of Priam's son Lykaon, pleading with Achilles to spare his life and accept ransom. Achilles is unyielding:

> *Friend ... why do you lament like this? ...*
> *Do you not see how handsome and tall I am?*
> *Of a noble father I am, and born of a goddess.*
> *Yet over me, too, hangs death and mighty fate.*
> *There will be a dawn, an evening or mid-day*
> *when my life, too, will be taken away ...*

Now handsome and tall (μεγας), tomorrow mighty, mightily stretched out (μεγας μεγαλωστι τανυσθεις, XVIII: 26). A common destiny puts the slayer and the slain on the same level. Death brings them together.

We hear the same contrast of antithetical states in Book XVI. Apollo strikes Patroklos (this is the only instance when a god directly strikes a lethal blow to a hero) and blows off Achilles' helmet worn by Patroklos to the ground, under the horses' feet:

> *and the plumes were smeared*
> *with blood and dust.*
> *But in former times it was not permitted*
> *that this horse-hair crest would be smeared with dust*
> *but, instead, it protected the head and brow*
> *of a godlike man, Achilles.*

Then and now: a complete reversal. Similarly, with the slaying of Hektor (Book XXII). Zeus loved him (διιφιλος) but could in no way stop him now from meeting his fate. Hektor, seeing his death approaching:

> *... [Zeus and Apollo] in former times*
> *were eager to protect me from harm.*
> *But now my doom is coming upon me.*

Soon, "godlike" Hektor is being dragged behind Achilles' chariot:

> *...his head lay all in the dust,*
> *the head that was before so fair.*

The godlike hero now on the ground, covered in mud. Hekabe laments him:

> *... [The Trojans] greeted you as a god.*
> *Their greatest glory was you to them*
> *while you were alive. But now death and fate are upon you.*

Andromache grieves for her dead husband and pities Astyanax who

> *Before, on the knees of his father,*
> *he was eating only marrow and the rich fat of sheep.*
> *... Now, having lost his dear father, he will suffer many woes.*

Scenes of painful and incomprehensible dissonance between "then" and "now" are numerous in a poem dealing with death. But such scenes are not limited to dying heroes. The hero, living, may find himself in contradictory states of mind from one day to the next. Thus, in Book VII, Hektor and Aias are fighting "like flesh-rending lions and wild boars." The whole conflict between the two armies is, at this point, focused on the duel between these two heroes. But then night comes. It is as if the sun's revolution brings about a complete turn-around of the psychological frame of each warrior and a radical change in their relationship. Tomorrow they will fight again, but now:

> *Let us give each other fine gifts*
> *so that Achaeans and Trojans will speak of us thus:*
> *'Even though they fought in soul-devouring strife*
> *they parted bound by friendship.'*

These are irreconcilable states, yet they exist side-by-side within each individual. The ravenous lion is bound to its pray by a deep alliance that identifies killer with victim and *vice versa*. It could be said that the lion kills its victim because it loves it. The relationship of gods to humans is, at times, no less contradictory: Hektor, Sarpedon, Patroklos, and Achilles are all loved by Zeus, yet he *plans* their death himself (Book XV). To say that Zeus loves them because they are doomed (Griffin, 1980) is only half the story.

The capacity of enemies to also be close friends, the ease with which the relationship can flip around, is further brought out in the encounter between Glaukos and Diomedes in Book VI. At one point they are about to destroy each other ("Come closer so that you will, sooner, meet your doom"), and at the next the same two are old friends exchanging gifts.

The discord between different human situations in time is not the only discord experienced. The following scene from the funeral of Patroklos, in Book XXIII, depicts another type of disharmony which is not temporal but is, rather, one between two levels of reality, or between *wish/dream/phantasy* on the one hand, and external reality on the other. Achilles, before lifting Patroklos onto the pyre, stops for a moment, gazing at the wine-dark sea, and cuts a golden lock from his hair that he had grown long as a gift intended for the river Spercheios upon returning home. His father had prayed to Spercheios for his son's return promising that Achilles would offer him a holy hecatomb and shear his hair for him:

> *Thus prayed the old man, but you did not fulfill his wish.*
> *Now, therefore, since I am not returning to my dear native land I*
> *would offer my hair to heroic Patroklos to take it with him.*

The future turning out to be different from what had been hoped it would be is stressed, here, in one line:

Spercheios, it was for a different favor (αλλως) that my father had prayed ...

The clash between dream and reality is, further, poignantly shown when Achilles falls asleep on the seashore and the image of dead Patroklos appears to him, his exact likeness. When Achilles tries to hold him, however, he discovers that there is nothing there, only vapor, and he suddenly wakes up bewildered and confronted with his irretrievable loss (XXIII: 62-107). What inhabits the space of dreams contrasts sharply with the objects residing in the space of reality.

In the episode of the lock of hair, Achilles is scanning the sea as he is cutting his lock. He is looking, across the Aegean, towards the coast on the other side, Phthia, knowing that he will never cross over that distance. The ritual offer will not be made "there" but "here." And it will not be an offer of celebration to honor life, but a funeral offer in honor of the dead. This alludes to another kind of contrast, one that is defined primarily by *space*. It is brought out with painful clarity in Iphition's "epitaph" (XX: 389-392):

*Here you lie, son of Otrynteus, of all men most remarkable.
Here is your death, but your birth is on Lake
Gygaea, where your father's domain lies,
next to Hyllos, full of fish, and the whirling Hermos.*

The physical distance from the place of birth, the geographic "otherness" of the place of death, intensifies the emotional rupture and the unbridgeable distance that separates the living from the dead.

Space fragmentation is a frequent reference, in the *Iliad*, as it appears associated with the motif of "dying far away from home." Thus Patroklos, in Book XI, looking at the wounded Achaeans pities them saying:

*Ah you wretched men, leaders and lords of the Danaans,
thus were you destined, far away from friends and native land
to feed with your white fat the swift dogs in Troy.*

Achilles mourns Patroklos who "perished very far from his own land." (XVIII: 99). And Achilles, himself, in answer to the immortal steed, Xanthos, who prophesies his imminent death, says:

*Well I know it myself that my death will destroy me here,
far away from my dear father and mother.*

Such emphasis on the "alien" quality of the place of death reflects the feeling that the living space is splintered and death is always *elsewhere*. Man is permanently conscious of the presence of an *other* place, the place of absence, the space of death.

Corresponding to this, however, there is the consciousness of a place that is inaccessible to man: This is the space of immortality inhabited by the gods. Human consciousness is itself splintered, turned at the same time towards death and towards immortality. This is the most radical kind of fragmentation. The gods are in an antithetical relationship to humans. They do not die and are free from suffering:

> *For this is how the gods have woven the thread for wretched mortals,*
> *that they should live in sorrow; but they themselves are free of cares*
> (XIV: 525-6).

Because gods experience no existential fragmentation they are not – they cannot be – tragic. The tragic arises in the juxtaposition of two opposing fragments, at their interface. The tragic in man becomes manifest when the hero attempts to transcend his humanity. It is the moment of his transcendence and his demise at the same time. Apollo cautions Diomedes:

> *Reflect now, son of Tydeus, and pull back.*
> *Do not believe yourself to be equal to gods*
> *since never is the race of immortal gods*
> *equal to that of men who walk on earth* (V: 440-2).

The overlooking or disregarding the chasm that separates gods and men represents a sort of metaphysical violence that brings disaster. Thus, in Book XVIII, Achilles, following the death of Patroklos ("my very own self"), is grieving his mortal destiny and wishing that his immortal mother had stayed in the company of her peers and that his father would have taken a mortal bride instead (86-7). Underneath his wish that he had never been born there is his wish that such a co-mingling between divine and human had not taken place and had not given birth to a half-god destined to meet bitter death. It is such a mixture that is the cause of all suffering. This is, also, clearly implied in Zeus' words to the two immortal horses (XVII: 443-5):

> *Ah luckless pair, Why did we give you to king Peleas*
> *who is mortal, while you are ageless and immortal?*
> *Was it so that you should have sorrows together with miserable*
> *humans?*

For Hegel (2006), when the Absolute enters the sphere of temporality tragic self-divisions and powerful collisions follow. The attempt at symbiosis between mortal and divine represents for George Steiner (1996) an event of aggression and can only lead to a more painful insight into the abyss that separates the two. Yet, it would seem that humans are unable to resist the pursuit of such insight into their existential fragmentation, regardless of the tragic cost.

It could be said, in conclusion, that tragic consciousness emerged out of the chasm that opened up with the emergence of *mind*, of thought, positioned opposite the body. The fractured, dis-articulated human being came, then, to be at the mercy of the various manifestations of that basic rift (temporal, spatial, and metaphysical).

THE TRAGIC ACT

The tragic, as the fragmentary nature of being and the co-existence of contradictory and irreconcilable states within human consciousness, is the background of all action in the *Iliad*. It forms a connecting thread that runs through the narrative and provides its underlying structure. Tragic consciousness becomes manifest in tragic action, and it is tragic action that gives the *Iliad* its profoundly tragic character. In an attempt to gain some understanding of the nature of the tragic act in the Epic we shall focus on two pivotal scenes in the *Iliad*, the scene in which Achilles learns of the death of Patroklos, in Book XVIII, and the scene of Achilles encounter with king Priam in the last Book.

Book XVIII begins with a reference to an uncanny acceleration of the flow of time: Antilochos, bringing the news of Patroklos' death, finds Achilles "reflecting in his mind what has in fact already taken place." The present is already past. Events will unfold rapidly from now on in a precipitous forward movement which telescopes time and brings the future to the present. Schadewaldt (1965) underlines the fact that Homer's world is governed by the principle of the presence of the future. The hero lives his future in the present. And, insofar as the future signifies death, death is the kernel of all action in the *Iliad*.

Using Aristotle's concepts characterizing tragic *mythos*, we could say that Patroklos' death represents a radical reversal of the situation (*peripeteia*) at this point, and brings about – of necessity – the painful recognition (*anagnorisis*) by Achilles of what has been until now inconceivable to him (or latent), a recognition which is accompanied by suffering (*pathos*). Achilles had prayed to Zeus, who decides the destiny of mortals with his two Urns, that the Achaeans should suffer a cruel defeat as punishment for Agamemnon's insult to Achilles' honor. His wish was granted! These things have come to pass exactly as he had prayed, Thetis says. Why weep then? Yes, the Olympian has kept his promise, Achilles admits, but "Where is my pleasure in this?" Once again, we are face-to-face with a divided antithetical reality. Zeus had granted half of Achilles' wish, but denied the other half (as he did with regard to Patroklos' foray, XVI: 250). Something has gone wrong. The Achaeans without Achilles' help were, indeed, defeated and humiliated, as Achilles had asked, but the fallen dead now include Patroklos as well. And Patroklos is "my own self," Achilles bemoans. Indeed something has gone wrong, the outcome that was hoped for has been turned upside down and Achilles' rage ended up directed against himself (by the death of his double). This was the result of a mistaken aim by Achilles, a "missed target" (the literal meaning of Aristotle's tragic *hamartia*[30], a metaphor borrowed from hunting). Achilles had committed an error in judgment, realizing it too late. His error, we might say, was his failure to comprehend that wishes can only be *partly* fulfilled, perhaps because the wisher himself is only a part, a fragment of reality. Limited. Objects are separate, outside the individual's control, and so can be lost. Division, a schism at the heart of being, is an ontological *a priori*. Achilles' hybristic narcissistic omnipotence blinded him. He is not the carrier of *hamartia*; he *is hamartia*, an anomalous co-mingling of the divine and the human.

But the *peripeteia* of Patroklos' death forces on Achilles another recognition. Patroklos was his "double" and so his death, wearing Achilles' own armor and riding his own immortal steeds, puts Achilles inescapably in front of his own death in a direct, immediate "face-to-face" confrontation with himself which had never occurred before this moment. Achilles has known all along about his early death, but now he *sees* it, he *lives* it; it is no longer something that he has been told. As he is gazing at the dead body of Patroklos, a "black cloud of grief covered him" – a poetic simile alluding to the moment of death. He "lay in dust outstretched, mighty in his might," his mother lamenting over him, holding his head. This is as if he is already dead. Achilles' death is not part of the tale told in the *Iliad*, but this explicit "flash-forward" scene well illustrates Schadewaldt (1965)'s remark that, in the *Iliad*, the present always foreshadows the future. Achilles says that he cannot remain among the living if he does not kill Hektor, but, if he kills Hektor, his own death is certain to follow straight away. Thus, from this point on, nothing can stop Achilles' determined advance towards death.

With his knowledge enhanced with these insights into his inherent *hamartia*, his limits, and his mortality, Achilles can now exclaim: "Would that strife and bitter anger perish from among gods and men!"

In the epic universe, this is the moment of transformation, when a mere mortal, a "vain burden upon the earth," transcends his nature to become a hero. Necessity no longer constrains nor determines the individual's actions as he now freely *chooses* his destiny in an act of tragic heroism. The action is tragic because it attempts a leap over the metaphysical gap of existence. Death is now accepted and pursued resolutely as an act of the individual Will and as a means of the ultimate self-realization of a whole and authentic being (Heidegger). Achilles embraces his death not passively submitting to it, but in a dialogue with his fate. "My death will I accept, whenever Zeus and the other immortal gods wish to bring it to pass," he repeats (XVIII: 115; XXII: 365). To the speaking immortal horse, Xanthos, prophesying his imminent day of doom, Achilles replies:

> *'Well I know it myself that it is my fate to perish here,*
> *far from my dear father and mother. But, even so,*

---

[30] *Hamartia* is usually translated in English as "tragic flaw."

> *I will not end before I give the Trojans their fill of war.'*
> *He spoke, and with a cry he drove his single-cloven horses out to the front.*

This resolute movement towards the final act, knowing that, in the end, all is lost, attests to the greatness of the hero at the point of his most profound fragility. The "I," having recognized its fundamental fragmentation and limitations that condemn it to be always "missing the mark," is now elevated onto another plane, where it affirms its mortality in a terminal act of heroic *euchos*:

> *And now, since countless are the fates of death that beset us,*
> *which no mortal can escape or avoid,*
> *let us go forward, either giving glory to someone, or someone to us.*

These are Sarpedon's words to Glaukos (XII: 326-8). And "god-like" Hektor, the "shepherd of peoples," he who was once succored by Zeus, knows that he is now about to meet his fate:

> *But let me not perish without a struggle and without glory,*
> *but by accomplishing something great that will be heard of*
> *by men yet to be.*

And so, the hero, by his tragic act that affirms his temporality, passes on to the timelessness of the immortal song.

Let us now look at the scene of the encounter between Achilles and old Priam in Book XXIV. Although there have been dissenting voices as to its authenticity (notably, Wilamowitz-Möllendorf, 1920), there is convincing internal evidence that this Book not only forms an integral part of the original composition but represents the very climax of the Epic's narrative movement (see Chapter One). The events recounted here provide the grounds of the psychological coherence and the organic unity of the whole tale.

Achilles is undoubtedly a most complex character, but his harshness and cruelty are a constant feature of his image as presented to us. We are told that he is in no way "of sweet temperament or of gentle mind, but of most fierce disposition" (XX: 467-8). He is likened to a lion or to a wolf and is described as hard, pitiless, and unrelenting as Death. Small wonder then that Hekabe tries, in vain, to dissuade Priam from going to meet this ruthless man. And Priam's journey to Achilles' tent is indeed a sort of *nekyia*, a visit to the House of Death to retrieve Hektor's body. Achilles receives Priam with awe, seeing him as a man "possessed by dark blindness." He knows that death awaits him in the hands of Priam's son. Priam is definitely the enemy, the king of the enemy barbarian people, whose other son has slain dear Patroklos. How can we explain, then, the sudden and unexpected change in Achilles' character in what follows?

Achilles – until now "unbending as iron" – listens to the old man kneeling in front of him, reminding him of his father, speaking of the endless sorrows that he has endured, his many sons slain by Achilles' murderous hands. And now, these same terrifying hands touch the old man gently and raise him, "*pitying*" (οικτειρων) his white head, while the two break in loud lament for the dear persons they have both lost. The two unyielding enemies now united in sharing their human destiny and the universality of human suffering. "Ah unhappy man, many are the evils that you have endured in your heart," Achilles says compassionately to Priam. He bemoans his own sort, being in Troy, so far away from his native land, "bringing woes to you and to your children." And then, Achilles, who had vowed that dogs and birds would devour Hektor's rotting flesh, orders the servants to bathe and anoint the dead body, and he himself lifts Hektor laying him on a bier, thereby commencing *himself* Hektor's funeral rites. For Lesky (1966), the events of the last Book represent the culmination of the *Iliad* and the starting point of the Western conception of humanity.

Aristotle believed that tragedy is superior to epic poetry because of the more "concentrated" nature of its story, which gives it more unity. The remarkably concentrated dense focus of Book XXIV and its tightly woven dynamic pattern unquestionably brings it very close to tragedy.

As a result of experiences precipitated by the death of Patroklos (Book XVIII), Achilles has come to know the limitations of human existence and that, ultimately, the arrows of hatred return to the self. He has experienced death in a direct, personal way and recognizes and accepts the inevitability and universality of human doom. The lucid recognition of these truths brings about a transformation in the character of the man who was, until now, harsh and unyielding as iron. He recognizes the Other as an image – indeed a fragment – of himself, with whom he shares the common human suffering and mortal destiny. This profound change leads to Achilles' *metabasis* towards a position of acceptance of the Other, accompanied by a feeling of genuine compassion and sharing the Other's pain. His former rage (μηνις) has been transformed into pity (ελεος, οικτος) – a process of *katharsis* of primitve hatred. He looks at Priam with marvel (θαυμαζειν), feeling regret and pity for a man, like himself, who did not deserve so many ills.

Thus, if the hero's tragic act in Book XVIII was his acceptance and embrace of death, his tragic act here, in the last Book, is his acceptance of the Other as part of the self in the community of suffering. This act is no less "heroic" than the act of embracing death. Although it departs from the conventional heroic *ethos* of achieving *kleos* in battle, it is nevertheless an act of tragic heroism equal to that of *kleos*. The aim of both acts is to bridge the gap at the core of being.

It seems, then, that the evolution of events in these two key scenes, in Book XVIII and Book XXIV, follows a certain intrinsic pattern that we could characterize as tragic. It is a pattern that expresses the inner logic of tragedy. As a result of unexpected situational reversals, the hero comes to recognize certain basic truths regarding the fragmentary and contradictory nature of reality. These have to do with mortality and the inevitability of human error. The "I" is constituted and defined by these two conditions. The consciousness of death, as a personal fact, creates time by drawing a future event into the present and making it actual; death creates time by destroying it. Error, as an inherent quality of human affairs, signifies that human projects are doomed to miss their aim because of the segmental and multifocal nature of reality. This is what led to Hegel (2006)'s conception of tragedy as a conflict between two *equal* "rights" or truths. The one that prevails is always bound to be wrong because it is only one-sided. Each of two contradictory ethical forces is just and at the same time unjust insofar as each can only attain its aim by suppressing the other.

The acquisition of this double insight brings about a transformation of the hero and impels him towards tragic action. The hero's tragic act is an attempt to transcend fragmentation by accepting and embracing the Other, the Other in its dual manifestation: the Other as Death, and the Other as the Other subject. The tragic act, accordingly, takes two forms: the typical heroic *kleos* in meeting one's death, and the compassionate *oiktos* towards the suffering Other subject. What makes the transcendental leap to embrace the Other possible is the recognition that death and the Other subject are inalienable parts of the self (death or non-being is a property of my being, and the Other subject is, as I am, part of the original One).

Tragic heroism breaks the chain of necessity. In the *Iliad*, Agamemnon's seizure of Briseis started a causal chain of events that followed each other of necessity: Achilles' anger, his appeal to Zeus for the Achaeans' defeat in battle, Patroklos' falling in the fighting, Achilles' avenging his death by killing Hektor, Achilles' death which is to follow of necessity. But a freely determined act of *kleos* or *oiktos* can abolish the absolute rule of inexorable *Ananke* and permit the emergence of tragic Free Will.

Yet the tragic act is not an act of triumph. It is done with the sad recognition of man's insignificance in the order of things, of the inevitability and universality of suffering and of the forces of Thanatos that unite us all, victors and victims alike. The tragic act is a product of what Melanie Klein called the "depressive position." The *Epic of Ilion* ends not in triumph but in sorrowful mourning shared by the two camps. The tragic act is an act of heroic sadness.

We may note at this point that the principal aim of psychoanalysis is, indeed, to assist the individual to recognize the multiple levels of fragmentation of her consciousness and to support her efforts towards accepting or tolerating the Other, both the Other as death as well as the Other as the Unconscious/the Other I. This would tend to break the chain of compulsive repetitiveness of neurotic living.

CONCLUDING REMARKS

In portraying the forces involved in life's combat, their interaction, mutual influence, and actualization in the final ascendancy of humane feeling, the *Iliad* created the inner structure of what was, later, to become, classical tragedy. It outlined the dynamic evolution of these forces as they shape human action, and depicted with exquisite poignancy the deeper impact of the sudden and unexpected acquisition of painful insights. In that sense, the *Iliad* can be considered to be an *Urtragödie*. It tells of man's heroic attempt to transcend himself with the full knowledge that the success of his endeavor signifies his defeat.

Unavoidably, the ethical question is pivotal in the *Iliad*. What humans *do* following their encounter with the tragic, how they incorporate it into their being, is at the root of tragic *ethos*.

And so, what of the bard and *his* act – the poetic act? For Aristotle, poetry, insofar as it deals with what *might* happen, with mankind's universal aspirations, is deeply philosophical. And, insofar as all philosophy can be said to be fundamentally ethics, the poet partakes of the *ethos* of the tragic hero in his task of transcending metaphysical fragmentation, by assembling the fragments of existence and bridging the gaps of time and of generations with his immortal *aoidé*.

Epilogue
ον φωνήεν

It is beyond doubt that Homer fashioned the inner landscape of Western man. It might be said that the very grammar of the Homeric Epics determined Western man's epistemological, social, and psychological universe, and articulated the basic categories by which this universe can be understood and talked about.

Following the Poet, we have undertaken a brief journey in his world, choosing to briefly stop at certain turns of the road, and we must now ask what, if anything, determined such a choice. Scanning over these random stops we may discern a common dynamic that characterizes all those instants. It seems that they all tell of a transition, a *metabasis*, a translocation from one state of being to another. They are all *metaphoric* in the strict sense of the word and they define the fundamental polarities in human experience. Thus, we followed a *metabasis* of the hero from a sense of ruthless omnipotence to a compassionate awareness of human limitations and mortality. We listened to the poet's own belief that life's unendurable pains are transubstantiated in song through the *metabasis* operated by the primal metaphor. We saw the hero transposed from sleeping dream to the dream of wakefulness. And we followed him in his *metabasis* to the world of the dead and back again to the living – living with the shadows of the dead in thought. We finally saw him spanning the gap over the fragments of his existence in the tragic struggle to hold onto both sides of an abyss. In all of this endless Herakleitian flow, we recognize the fundamental categories of man's self-definition, a definition based on conflict and transition.

The never-ending movement along these basic axes can be seen as a manifestation of a primary *metabasis*, that from the primordial unit (One) of an undifferentiated, all-encompassing reality (fused mother-infant) to a state of differentiation and separateness in which the individual autonomous "I" has broken off – both physically and psychologically – from the One to give rise to Two. This basic process of fusion—differentiation in human development, encoded as it is in our phylogenetic unconscious, has been the source of mythical cosmological beliefs and of metaphysical speculation. The various axes of movement described above are best understood as components of that basic process. In retrospect it would seem, therefore, that the choice to focus on those particular scenes of the epics may not have been entirely at random.

The central question that emerges from the dynamics of the basic process of differentiation is the nature of the *relation* between the two resulting existential poles, that is, between the two (unstable) states – a relation itself in constant evolution. This question eventually revolves around the issue of continuity versus discontinuity and it gets tangled in the webs of paradox since the relation implicates categorically distinct states. This may be the principal reason for the indeterminate, indefinite, and fluctuating nature of the link between the two sides. The situation is further complicated by the fact that the movement from one state to the other involves *loss*, the loss of something that, in the evolutionary movement, must be left behind. Owing to the categorical gap that distinguishes the new state from the old, the nascent "I" finds it enormously difficult to accept the loss. Thus, there is an unremitting drive to reverse the process of differentiation and to remain within the security of the "familiar" that characterizes the original state. This results in a back-and-forth oscillation of the "I" between One and Two, between fusion and differentiation, between megalomanic omnipotence and acceptance of human limits, between a bodily "I" and a mental "I", between dream/phantasy and external reality, between inexorable time and timelessness, between living creatively and living in death. The dynamic of this perpetual oscillation makes George Steiner (1996) astutely observe that, in fact, "in the laws of human physics, fission is fusion."

But, who among our contemporaries would be more skilled to discern and follow the thread of the labyrinthine inter-lacings of human fissional-fusional states than the great Master of keen vision, Jorge Luis Borges? In a short story entitled *The Other* the poet finds himself sitting on a park bench with a younger man whom, when the latter starts singing a song, he recognizes as being himself, but situated in another time and place. Borges admits his discomfort: he would much prefer to be alone rather than with his double. The situation is imbued with terror. Is Borges dreaming the Other, or is he himself the Other's dream? He forgets that he remembers his other self, as "memory is often like forgetfulness." He tries to calm himself saying that, in any case, when one wakes up one always meets oneself again. But what if the dream never ends? He feels a parental wave of love for this Other – "dearer to me than a child of my own flesh and blood." What is terrifying is the realization that although the same, the two are different. Time "does not pass without leaving a mark ... We are too different, yet too alike." He finally concludes that the encounter was real but "the other man spoke to me in a dream, which was why he could forget me; I spoke to him while I was awake, and so I am still tormented by the memory." Unquestionably, the same park bench existed in two times and two places. But the Greek who said that *Yesterday's man is not today's* was right, says Borges. In the end, "our clear obligation is to accept the dream, as we have accepted the universe and our having been brought into it." We must accept that reality has many faces (Borges, 1998, pp. 411-417).

The chief product of the categorical leap from One to Two in all of its component dimensions (the *metabases* mentioned above) is the sense of Time. Time is generated by that movement which is driven by the forces of Life (Eros) and carries within it the germ of Death (Thanatos). The gap separating the two sides from which Time emerges, the gap that it occupies, is the basic interval of time. The perpetual back-and-forth random oscillation between the two poles that define that space lends Time its characteristic elasticity. Time has, accordingly, been the *leitmotif* of all the Homeric scenes we have considered thus far. We saw the Time of mortality and compassion; the soothing Time of narration and song; the Time of frightful and joyful discovery of the old that is new; the Time of shadows and of memory; the Time of tragic fragmentation and of heroic transcendence. The constant feature in all these manifestations of temporality, the ground from which they arise, is the experience of loss. Loss is constitutive of Time. And, since loss is an essential characteristic of the Herakleitian flow that constitutes man's nature, we can see that man's nature is inherently temporal.

Loss, as a radical change of the status quo of living matter, is traumatic to the "I" which mobilizes powerful defenses to deal with it. The complex manoeuvres that the "I" undertakes in order to come to terms with loss are part of what we call "mourning." Because, as mentioned above, loss is never fully accepted since the original One is never given up, mourning becomes an indissociable element of all human action. If mourning is productive, that is if it succeeds in containing the overwhelming depressive anxieties inundating the "I," and the so-called depressive position has been achieved, then loss is more or less endured and the reaction to it is sadness. If this fails, the result is depression. For Winnicott (1975), managing the depressive position is "the problem of life" (p. 276). It is a problem that pertains to the problematic of Being, in the dialectic of One-Two. Only after this is grappled with can the "I" proceed to confront the oedipal dynamic of Three. But it would seem that the fundamental task of life is dealing with loss.

Mourning, sadness, and regrets are part of all the scenes that we examined and constitute the emotional ambiance and affective background of the hero's actions. It is not surprising that θρηνος is central to tragedy, an art form that grew out of the Great Epics. The altar at the center of the orchestra orients the action around the body of the mutilated wine-blood god, or around the body of the dead hero. Lamentation ceremonies for the divinized hero or the humanized god may well have been the origins of tragedy. In the space defined by the primal undifferentiated chorus on the one hand and the isolated hero that broke off and away from it on the other the primordial conflict between the fusional magnetism of Eros and the schismatic disruption of Thanatos is enacted. The paradox is that, in that arena, the fragmenting, dis-uniting forces of Thanatos work in the service of Eros, of Life. The individual *must* maintain itself in differentiating conflict with the social group; the gap separating them *must* be preserved: only then can the hero's pre-ordained defeat lead to transcendence and to his acquisition of subjecthood and personal identity. But that requires the hero to act. The act is never morally neutral, never innocent. It actualizes the hero's *hamartia* and concretizes the conflict. Western man after Homer has not been able to understand himself outside the primary category of conflict, a conflict that is creative but remains fundamentally insoluble. Through the human act the Hegellian Absolute, the moral universe engaged by the individual, suffers a self-division that leads to its affirmation only through a tragic collapse.

In the epic, the dynamic confrontation of the polarities is immeasurably more violent than in tragedy since the entire action is internal, exclusively re-enacted in the internal stage of the listener. There is no *dran* (δραν) in the physical world – the drama is only in the private recesses of the individual psyche, and here the "orchestral space" is vaster and more richly populated.

Much ink has been spent on the second choral ode in Sophokles' *Antigone*. Of all creatures, we are told there, none is *deinoteron* (more *deinos*) than man. Δεινός carries a complex meaning that contains traces of the original ambiguity of words that made them capable of conveying opposite senses. Thus it indicates "awe-inspiring," "marvelous," "terrifying," "mighty," "strange," "wondrous." The poet intended all of these senses, leaving the choice to the listener in his various states of mind. From our perspective, what makes man *deinoteron* of all living creatures is his unique manner of dealing with his defining conflict with the external world: since the conflict cannot be resolved or circumvented it is *incorporated*; it is now re-located in the internal world where it becomes constitutive of the "I." By means of an act – an act of tragic heroism, we might say – the "I" achieves self-realization through the affirmation of division and fragmentation. Man affirms himself against the opposing world by assuming the opposition *himself*. The now internalized polarization between the different modalities of the primal conflict of differentiation, namely, omnipotence - limitations (divine - human), body - mind, dream - reality, living - dead, determine man's mode of being. But the momentous significance of this internalization is that it inaugurates and establishes man's *reflective* capacity, his unique ability to be conscious of himself as existing. In the act of internalization man becomes the container of insuperable divisions – indeed he *becomes* those divisions. The incorporated divisions now erected within the self are subtended by the essential division of the "I" as subject and as object to itself – an "I" existing as a living divided consciousness.

Now we can see why epic poetry can be more disturbing or produce more turbulence in the psyche than drama, since it enters the internal world of the listener *directly*, making un-mediated contact with the inner conflictual polarities (see e.g., Odysseus' tears while listening to Demodokos). The mediating space of an external stage and characters, the illusion of an external conflict involving identified persons acting (*dran*) out there, is by-passed. All motion, here, is internal, undiluted or unmitigated e-motion to be suffered in silence. In drama, on the other hand, there is always an imaginary dialogue going on between the spectator and the actor. In epic poetry, the "spectator" follows the hero's movements with eyes shut, as it were, mirroring the blind bard.

The great Homeric Epics were the distillate of a long tradition of oral poetry whose early beginnings can be traced beyond the boundaries of Hellas. Our review of some key scenes of these epics isolated certain basic categories by which Western man tries to understand himself. We suggested that these different axes of human experience are reflections or elaborations of a primal process of evolution of separate entities that grew out of an original undifferentiated One. The Homeric Epics present us with one of the earliest – if not the earliest – formulation of this principle, its manifold vicissitudes and the eventual tragic impasse to which it may lead. That which poetic insight outlined in the eighth century, philosophy took up as its main focus less than two hundred years later. The pre-Socratics made the question of the One and the Many their main concern. As always, insight precedes science, or knowledge rationally-arrived-at. It is of significance that it was poetry, first, that expressed the need to speak of the primordial enigma of Being. It may well be that it was indeed that primal, fundamental question itself that gave rise to poetry.

This, now, leads us to consider the relation of the word (επος), of speech, to man's primordial conflict of differentiation. Let us return to *Antigone*'s second stasimon. The chorus sings the achievements that testify to man's awe-inspiring nature:

και φθεγμα και ανεμοεν φρονημα ... εδιδαξατο
(and speech and windy thought he learned for himself).

This seemingly innocent phrase conceals a powerful metaphysical statement to which we can only allude here. Thought, is a windy creature, born of wind, of the air of breath. The air of breath produces vocalization, speech: φθεγμα. It is speech that lays down the mind's conceptual avenues, delineates the mental map. But speech, being a windy thing, will fashion a mental map that is unpredictably mutable and forever unstable.

Let us look at the chief manifestation of man's δεινοτης, namely φθεγμα. This seems to be an onomatopoietic word designating the origin of speech through the production of sound by blowing air out and against resistance. The resistance is created first by the lower lip (φ) and then by the tongue (θ) affixed to the upper teeth, thereby obstructing the exit of air. For the moment, no vowel is produced. Then the accumulated tension of the obstructed air is released to reach the world outside and thereby produce a vowel – and an ον φωνήεν, a speaking being that has broken out of the solipsism of a narcissistic existence. It is possible that the first vowel (φθεγμα) was εεεεεε... The letter ε ψιλον was of special significance to the Hellenes as we witness it in its inscription above the entrance of Apollo's temple at Delfoi. Be that as it may, what retains our attention here is the particular mechanism of production of sound – at least in Greek – and its significance within that culture. What is germane to our discussion is that, in this schema, man in his δεινοτης affirms his existence and his presence in the world through an act of speech that is characterized by self-opposition, self-contradiction, and ambivalence. The air that comes from inside is projected out, but, with equal determination, it is stopped! Beyond designating the fundamental ambiguity of all language, it demonstrates the uniquely Greek characteristic of self-division that is at the root of tragedy and of the dialectic process. The Greek universe of discourse is formulated on the basis of *men ... de* (μεν ... δε: two opposite sides). But the mechanism of production of speech also illustrates the internalization of the conflict between the individual and the opposing world, to which we referred above. The opposition to one's actions now comes not from the outside, but from a counter-action posed by the individual herself, against herself, within herself.

We may now address the question of the "motive", the drive that led to the first vocalization. What impelled it? It is better, perhaps, to speak of "reasons," rather than "motives" here. The infant's first inarticulate "meaningful" sound arises in the void of the absent primary object, in the gap that appears following the rupture of the original unity in the process of differentiation. It is the infant's attempt to re-connect with the primary object, to recapture the lost state of Oneness. It reaches out to what is lost, it seeks to establish a link with it, and, soon, it *becomes* the absent object. It is the irony of human existence that we begin our life, as we end it, with an identity defined by absence. The infant's babble as a transitional object (Winnicott, 1971), emerging in the space of transition from One to Two, reconstitutes the original state of "being-one-with" mother. Language arises in the gap that follows the splitting of the One and speaks of loss; indeed language speaks the loss. And, as language shares the same space as time and speaks the loss which constitutes time, language fundamentally speaks time.

In Homer, the minstrel's words are the voice of the gods (θεσπις αοιδη). They are conveyed to the poet by the daughters of *Mnemosyne* and they speak what *is*. Being (ον) is thereby made present (παρον), in a Heideggerian listening. From a psychoanalytic perspective, the Ancients' divine Being and the source of all that *is*, from the infant's point of view, is the original mother of One-ness. She is the source of being and all sense of being derives from her. It is this "pure distilled uncontaminated female element" – Winnicott (1971) believes – that "leads us to *Being*, and this forms the only basis for self-discovery and a sense of existing." In his view, the original mother of undifferentiation is "the foundation of the experience of being." Accordingly, the infant's earliest driven vocalizations acquire their substance by speaking Being (i.e., by becoming), and rendering present, the absent Being of origins. The first "word," in naming the absent object and establishing Being, posits permanence, a core that endures. This sense of permanence will subsequently enable the growing "I" to engage in *Doing* and to become an agent of change.

In view of these considerations we see that, underlying the epic's articulation of the various *metabases* that we examined above, there is the primordial, fundamental, and immanent relation of the word (επος) to the basic differentiation process, the process that is expressed via these *metabases*. We may, thus, postulate a *phonetic imperative*, as a concept that refers to the infant's drive to establish, ground, and affirm its being through the vocal sound (φθεγμα). This is a testimony to man's δεινοτης. Heidegger asserts that "The being of man is founded on speech."

It would seem, however, that the linguistic roots of man's being are also the source of his existential paradoxes, contradictions and tragic impasses. This is so because the word is first enunciated as an affirmation of Being – naming Being. But the very act of naming it takes place at the moment of its loss (the loss of the original oneness with mother), and so the word names, at the same time, Being and its absence. Put differently: The word speaks Being in its primordial state in which it is not yet differentiated from non-Being. The word is, thus, a *shadow* of the primary object, designating both the object and its absence. As a consequence, man's identity, arising at the moment of separation from mother to become a distinct entity and being founded on speech, is a fluctuant and unstable identity. This is so, not only because of the oscillating nature of the differentiation process (fission-fusion), but also owing to the existential contradictoriness of the word.

The earliest speech of the child – the "first word" – is meta-phoric *to* Being, seeking to capture Being in its absence, naming simultaneously Being and non-Being. This *primal ambiguity* of the word, the ambiguity of primitive speech, is what renders it inherently poetic. It is what makes Heidegger affirm that the essence of poetry is the establishment of Being through words, and that "the Ur-speech is poetry as the foundation (*Stiftung*) of Being."

The creative development of the infant depends on its encounter with the contradiction of its origins. Drawing its sense of being by turning to the original source, the infant comes, inescapably, face-to-face with the element of non-being, of absence. The primal ambiguity bestows a radical "poeticity" on the growing "I" and provides the impetus for new developments. This basic poeticity, in the strict sense of creativity (*poiein*), allows the infant to turn away from a narcissistic engulfment in the undifferentiated One and to seek new objects of attachment in new directions, provided absence can be tolerated and the absent object mourned.

A need will now emerge, as part of an on-going process of mourning, to *tell the story* of an incomprehensible loss. Confronted with the paradoxical ambiguity of Being, the "I" will begin an interminable series of attempts to *relate* the two polarities of Being in their various manifestations, and to create meaning. We might call this the *narrative imperative* which is an evolution of the earlier phonetic imperative. The narrative imperative is in the service of meaning and represents a way of coming to terms with the primordial loss. Unlike the phonetic imperative which is narcissistically addressed to the original One of undifferentiation, the narrative imperative is turned outwards, towards the differentiated Other. Thus, the word creates a bridge towards the Other, both as absence-Death and as the Other "I." As such, the word ($\varepsilon\pi o\varsigma$) constitutes a tragic act (see Chapter Five). This would imply that all poetry is, fundamentally, a tragic act.

The narrative imperative speaks words of familiarity that have become unfamiliar, it speaks a maternal language that is now a foreign language, the language of the Other. In Rilke's words (*The Sonnets to Orpheus* I, 3):

> *Singing is a different kind of breath.*
> *A breath about nothing. A gust in god. A wind.*

This, incidentally, recalls Plato's notion of poetry as a "light and flighty thing" (*Ion*). Thus, speech retains forever its primordial, its inherent poetic essence which we will later call "symbolic." Like a *symbolon*, it constructs a bridge towards the One and *away from it*, a bridge between what is lost and what is yet to come, always suspended over a void, a gap, always "indicating" a lack. Symbols are monuments to lost objects and signposts of hope. And it is this that makes the psychoanalytic project possible. This project, using words in their primordial function, aims to navigate through the rough waters, the uncharted routes of the various *metabases*.

Only in humans can the sound produced by exhaling air become the mental representation of the absent object. First, it *is* the object, it speaks the object, then it speaks *of* the object and of its loss; it becomes the narrative of a journey, a journey that involves loss. It could be said that, fundamentally, all poetry speaks of loss, regardless of its surface structure. In the Homeric scenes that we reviewed we listened to the journey from omnipotence reserved only for the gods to human mortality and sorrow; from dreams and aspirations to the limitations and disappointments of a reality that is beyond human control; from the tranquil contentment of affectionate ties binding humans to cruel irrevocable separations. If the poet's words always name the loss – the loss of a mythical Oneness with the object - then all poetry is, ultimately, elegiac, permeated by a primeval sadness. This is explicit in some poets, not so in others. Rilke belongs to the former:

> *In the end, no longer do they need us,*
> *those taken away from us early.*
> *... But we, who need*
> *such great mysteries, from whose sorrow the soul's growth*
> *so often emanates: Could we be without them?*
> *(Duino Elegies 1)*

Or:

> *And yet, in the alert, warm animal, there is*
> *the weight and the worry of an enormous sadness.*
> *For it, too, is always imbued with what often*
> *overwhelms us, a memory...*
> *(Duino Elegies 8).*

The sorrows, or the grief (*Trauer*), of the great mysteries provide the motive force and the energy for the growth of the psyche, according to Rilke, and are, therefore, in the service of the life forces (Eros). Thus, the alert warm animal turns towards "the Open" always weighted down by the sadness of a memory.

In Euripides' *Bacchae* we have a unique case of a tragedy that reflects on its own nature. Here, poetry looks at itself. Pentheus' (the "*mourner*") tragic flaw was his inability to tolerate the primal ambiguity of Being, the contradictory nature of reality (represented by Dionysos). He was, thus, unable to be poetic. And, foreclosing the whole universe of his origins, he was unable to go through the experience of mourning the inescapable loss. Pentheus could not be poetic and, consequently, he could not mourn (πενθειν). The grief of loss of the original unity turns the child's words towards the world (the world as the Other), and the poet's "flying words" (επεα πτεροεντα) towards new gods (Heidegger). It was precisely that turn to new gods that was beyond Pentheus' capacity – his psychic growth was arrested and his death inevitable.

The infant poet's word, suspended between the object of phantasy and the reality of its absence, will now create a new order of reality. The poet's words speaking the voice of the Muse will also point towards new worlds. We recall that the Muses first sang to celebrate the birth of the New Order of the Olympians. The creation of the new order, under the pushing forward of Eros, is unstoppable, as we see in the *Bacchae*. But the driving forces (Dionysos) are also forces of disorder. For Hölderlin (1996), the poet is the wine-god's priest, caught in that dionysian cosmic "in-between": between order and disorder, between divine and human, between fusion and mutilation, between Being and Absence; permanently hovering over a destitute space, in times of need (*dürftiger Zeit*).

The eternal appeal of the Homeric Epics, their strange familiarity despite the millennia that separate us from the sources of their composition, is the result of many and complex factors in mutual interaction. They are, unquestionably, the product and the embodiment of a many-layered *metabases* on social, intellectual and psychological planes. They are situated indeed between old and new gods. In the transition from the so-called Greek Dark Ages to the *logos* and tragic clarity of the Classical period, the Epics struggle to articulate a new language, a language that carries the old concepts (the old syntactical categories) to new territory. This imposes a strain, a certain deformation, on the Poet's speech, his thought and the flow of his tale, creating a narrative landscape that appears strange today and fits with difficulty into modern aesthetics. This compounds the multiplicity of other problems that challenge the modern reader. Perhaps, more than any other great poetry, the Homeric Epics voice the labor of the word to tame itself, to stay fixed in the air yet let itself be carried by the powerful gust of the wind of change.

The debate about whether the Epics were written down by their composer or not will probably never end: The poet's word will always resist being fixed down. But it is of the very essence of these Epics that they were born at the moment of the appearance of the Greek alphabet, at the exact time of the transition, confrontation, and conflict between the oral and the written word. Today, we read them as they were set to writing at the time of the Peisistratian recension. The creative primal ambiguity of the original word is largely lost: the unavoidable deficit of translation across time.

Over the centuries that followed the appearance of the Great Epics Western man never ceased to ponder the paradoxes and contradictions of one verb: *to be* – from Parmenides to Sartre. In a manner of speaking, the whole of language can be thought to have developed, syntactically and semantically, around this verb and in response to an imperative need to attach meaning to it – to construct an "argument" around it, to use the language of linguists. Thus, through words, man sought to tolerate and acquire a consciousness of: Being a fragment of a whole (or Being-in-fragments), Being-in-lack-of, Being-in-time. He struggled to develop a capacity for Being-in-Death (Being-with-Death), Being-in-thought, Being-with-the-Other. These are dimensions of Being that arise in response to loss and are present in an inchoate form in the first word uttered by a human (on the ontogenetic or phylogenetic scale). They manifest the "poietic" capacity of early language to "make" (ποιειν) the world, to endow it with Being, and allow it to differentiate into subjective and objective worlds that mingle and fall apart in an endless oscillation. Man, always at the "crossing of the two roads of his heart" (Rilke), lets himself be carried by the sounds of Apollo's lyre:

Gesang ist Dasein,

proclaims the poet. The Song is Being. Being-in-Song provides a link with the origins, establishing a continuity of being in the self as it traverses the various *metabases*, but, also, a continuity of being that extends beyond the individual, a continuity across generations. Being precedes the individual. The word as poietic *αοιδη* flies over and across to the Other, to the Other as Death, and beyond, to the Other human.

... *ινα ησι και εσσομενοισιν αοιδη*[31]

---

[31] ...so there may be a song for those that are yet to be.

Bibliography

Abraham, K. (1924). A Short Study of the Development of the Libido. In *Selected Papers in Psycho-Analysis* (1948), 418-501. London: Hogarth Press.
Adorno, T. (1967). *Prisms*. (S. Weber, Trans.). London: Spearman.
Adorno, T. (1973). *Negative Dialectics*. (B. Ashton, Trans.). New York: Routledge.
Akhtar, S. (2000). Mental pain and the cultural ointment of poetry. *International Journal of Psycho-Analysis, 81*, 229-243.
Arendt, H. (1977). *The Life of the Mind, Thinking*. New York: Harcourt Brace Jovanovich.
Aristotle. (1970). *Physics*, Book IV. (P. H. Wicksteed & F. M. Cornford, Trans.). Cambridge, MA: Harvard University Press.
Aristotle. (1995). *Poetics*. (S. Halliwell, Trans.). Cambridge, MA: Harvard University Press.
Arlow, J. (1986). Psychoanalysis and Time. *Journal of the American Psychoanalytic Association, 34*, 507-528.
Arvanitakis, K. (1998). Some thoughts on the essence of the tragic. *International Journal of Psycho-Analysis, 79*, 955-964.
Aulagnier, P. (1984). *L'apprenti-historien et le maître-sorcier*. Paris: P.U.F.
Beardsley, M. (1981). *Aesthetics*. Indianapolis: Hackett Publishing Co.
Bethe, E. (1914). *Homer. Dichtung und Sage*. Leipsig.
Bion, W. (1962a). The psycho-analytic study of thinking. *International Journal of Psycho-Analysis, 43*, 306-310.
Bion, W. (1962b). *Second Thoughts*. London: Heinemann.
Bion, W. (1977). *Seven Servants*. New York: Aronson.
Black, M. (1955). Metaphor. *Proceedings of the Aristotelian Society, LV*, 273-294.
Black, M. (1962). *Models and Metaphors*. Ithaca, NY: Cornell University Press.
Black, M. (1977). More about metaphor. *Dialectica, 31*, 431-457.
Borges, J. L. (1998). *Collected Fictions*. New York: Penguin.
Borges, J. L. (2000). Odyssey, Book Twenty-three. In *Selected Poems*, A. Coleman (Ed.). New York: Penguin.
Bowra, C. M. (1930). *Tradition and Design in the Iliad*. Oxford: Clarendon Press.
Bowra, C. M. (1962). Composition. In *A Companion to Homer*, A. Wace & F. Stubbings (Ed.). London: MacMillan.
Brenman, E. (1985). Cruelty and narrow-mindedness. In *Melanie Klein Today*, E. Bott Spillius (Ed.), 256-270. London: Routledge.
Brooks, C. (1947).*The Well Wrought Urn*. New York: Harcourt, Brace & World Inc.
Burkert, W. (1983). *Homo Necans*. (P. Bing, Trans.). Berkeley, CA: University of California Press.
Butcher, S.H. (1951). *Aristotle's Theory of Poetry and Fine Art*. New York: Dover Publications.
Cassirer, E. (1946). *Language and Myth*. (S. Langer, Trans.). New York: Dover Publications.
Castoriades-Aulagnier, P. (1975). *La violence de l'interprétation*. Paris: P.U.F.
Dante, A. (2002). *The Inferno*. (R. Hollander & J. Hollander, Trans.). New York: Anchor Books.

de Jong, I. J. F. (1995). Homer as literature: Some current areas of research. In *Homeric Questions*, J. P. Crielaard (Ed.). Amsterdam: J. C. Gieben.
de Jong, I. J. F. (2001). *A narrational commentary on the Odyssey*. Cambridge, U.K: Cambridge U. Press.
de M'Uzan, M. (1977). *De l'art à la mort*. Paris: Gallimard.
de Romilly, J. (1991). *Patience mon coeur*. Paris: Les Belles Lettres.
Devereux, G. (1978). Achilles' "suicide" in the *Iliad*. *Helios, 6*, 3-15.
Diels, H. & Kranz, W. (1956). *Die Fragmente der Vorsokratiker*. Berlin.
Eustathius (1960). *Commentarii ad Homeri Iliadem et Odysseam*. Hildesheim: G. Olms.
Fagles, R. (1991). *The Iliad*. New York, NY: Penguin Books.
Fagles, R. (1997). *The Odyssey*. New York, NY: Penguin Books.
Fenik, B. (1974). *Studies in the Odyssey*. Weibaden: F. Steiner Verlag.
Finley, J. Jr. (1978). *Homer's Odyssey*. Cambridge, MA: Harvard University Press.
Fränkel, H. (1986). The New Mood of the *Odyssey*. In *Homer*, H. Bloom (Ed.), 163-170. New York: Chelsea House.
Freud, S. (1905). *Three Essays on the Theory of Sexuality*. Standard Edition, 7, pp.123-242. London: Hogarth Press.
Freud, S. (1920). *Beyond the Pleasure Principle*. Standard Edition, 18, pp.14-155. London: Hogarth Press.
Freud, S. (1921). *Group Psychology and the Analysis of the Ego*. Standard Edition, 18, pp. 65-144. London: Hogarth Press.
Freud, S. (1925). *A Note upon the 'Mystic Writing-Pad'*. Standard Edition, 19, pp. 226-232. London: Hogarth Press.
Freud, S. (1940). *An Outline of Psycho-Analysis*. Standard Edition, 23, p. 139-207. London: Hogarth Press.
Gardner, J. & Maier, J. (Tr.). (1985). *Gilgamesh*. New York: Vintage Books.
Gadamer, H-G. (1975). *Truth and Method*. New York: Crossroad Publishing Co.
Geddes, W. D. (1878). *The Problem of the Homeric Poems*. London: MacMillan.
Goethe, W. (1962). *Faust*. New York: Bantam Books.
Green, A. (2000a). *Le temps éclaté*. Paris: Les éditions de minuit.
Green, A. (2000b). Science and science fiction. In *Clinical and Observational psychoanalytic research*, A. M. Sandler & R. Davies (Ed.). London: Karnac Books.
Griffin, J. (1980). *Homer on life and death*. Oxford: Oxford Univ. Press.
Hamilton, E. & Cairns, H. (1973). Timaeus. In *The Collected Dialogues of Plato*, 1151-1211. Princeton, NJ: Princeton University Press.
Hansen, W. (1997). Homer and the Folktale. In *A New Companion to Homer*, I. Morris & B. Powell (Ed.), 442-462. New York: Brill.
Hartocollis, P. (1983). *Time and Timelessness*. New York: I.U.P.
Hegel, G. W. F. (1967). *Philosophy of Right*. (T. M. Knox, Trans.). Oxford: Oxford University Press.
Hegel, G. W. F. (2006). *Lectures on the philosophy of religion*. Oxford: Oxford University Press.
Heidegger, M. (1949). *Existence and Being*. London: Vision Press; also, Chicago, IL: Henry Regnery Co.
Heidegger, M. (1962). *Being and Time*. (J. Macquarrie & E. Robinson, Trans.). New York: Harper & Row Publishers.
Herodotus (1981). *Historiae*. (A. D. Godley, Trans.). Cambridge, MA: Harvard University Press.

Hesiod (1950). *Theogony*. (H. G. Evelyn-White, Trans.). Cambridge, MA: Harvard University Press.
Heubeck, A. & Hoekstra, A. (1989). *A commentary on Homer's Odyssey*. Oxford: Clarendon Press.
Hölderlin, F. (1996). *Selected Poems and Fragments*. J. Adler (Ed.). London: Penguin.
Holland, N. (1999). Cognitive Linguistics. *International Journal of Psycho-Analysis, 80*, 357-363.
Homer. (1920). *Homeri Opera*. D. B. Munro, & T. W. Allen (Eds.). London: Oxford Classical Texts.
Isaacs, S. (1948). The structure and function of phantasy. *International Journal of Psycho-Analysis, 29*, 73-97.
Jaeger, W. (1973) *Paideia: The Ideals of Greek Culture*. Oxford: Oxford University Press.
Jakobson, R. (1987). *Language in Literature*. Cambridge, MA: Harvard University Press.
Johnson, M. (1987). *The Body in the Mind*. Chicago, IL: University of Chicago Press.
Καζαντζάκης, Ν. (2006). *Οδύσσεια*. Αθήνα: Εκδόσεις Καζαντζάκη.
Κακριδής, Ι. (1944). *Ομηρικές Έρευνες*. Αθήναι.
Κακριδής, Ι. (1985). *Το Μήνυμα του Ομήρου*. Αθήναι
Kant, I. (1929). *Critique of Pure Reason*. (N. Kemp Smith, Trans.). New York: St. Martin's Press.
Kirchhoff, A. (1879). *Die homerische Odyssee*. Berlin.
Kirk, G. S. (1970). *'The Bacchae' by Euripides*. Englewood Cliffs, NJ: Prentice Hall.
Kirk, G. S. & Raven, J. E. (1971). *The Presocratic Philosophers*. Cambridge, UK: Cambridge University Press.
Kirk, G. S. (1976). *Homer and the Oral Tradition*. Cambridge, UK: Cambridge University Press.
Klein, M. (1935). A contribution to the psychogenesis of manic-depressive states. *International Journal of Psycho-Analysis, 16*: 145-174.
Klein, M. (1948). *Contributions to Psychoanalysis*. London: Hogarth Press.
Klein, M. (1975). *The Writings of Melanie Klein*, Vol. 1. London: Hogarth Press, pp. 236-247.
Kristeva, J. (2000). From symbols to flesh. *International Journal of Psycho-Analysis, 81*: 771-787.
Lakoff, G. & Johnson, M. (1980). *Metaphors We Live By*. Chicago, IL: University of Chicago Press.
Lakoff, G. & Turner, M. (1989). *More than Cool Reason*. Chicago, IL: University of Chicago Press.
Lattimore, R. (2011). *The Iliad of Homer* (revised ed.). Chicago, IL: University of Chicago Press.
Lesky, A. (1966). *History of Greek Literature* (J. Willis & C. de Heer, Trans.). London: Hackett Pub.
Lewin, B. (1946). Sleep, the mouth and the dream screen. *International Journal of Psycho-Analysis. 29*, 224-234.
Lewin, B. (1973). *Selected Writings of B.D.Lewin*. New York: Psychoanalytic Quarterly Press.
Lewin, K. (1971). Metaphor, Mind and Manikin. *Psychoanalytic Quarterly, 40*, 6-39.
Longinus, (1990). *Περί Ύψους*. Ηράκλειον: Βικελαία Βιβλιοθήκη.
MacCary, W. T. (1982). *Childlike Achilles*. New York: Columbia University Press.
Marg, W. (1973). Zur Eigenart der Odyssee. *Antike und Abendland, 18*, 1-12.

Mattes, W. (1958) *Odysseus bei den Phâaken*. Wurtzburg,
Melnick, B. (1997). Metaphor and the theory of libidinal development. *International Journal of Psycho-Analysis, 78*, 997-1015.
Milner, M. (1957). *On Not Being Able to Paint*. London: Heinemann.
Mitchell, S. (2011). *The Iliad*. New York: Free Press.
Molière (1999). *Le bourgeois gentilhomme*. G. Couton (Ed.). Paris: Gallimard.
Morris, S. (1997). Homer and the Near East. In *A New Companion to Homer*, I. Morris & B. Powell (Ed.), 599-623. New York: Brill.
Most, G. W. (1989). The structure and function of Odysseus' *Apologoi*. In I.J.E. de Jong (Ed.), *Homer: critical assessments* (Vol III, 1999), 489-491. London: Routledge.
Muirden, J. (2012). *The Iliad*. Rewe, Devon, UK: Westfield Books.
Myres, J. N. L. (1932). The Last Book of the Iliad. *Journal of Hellenic Studies, 52*, 264-296.
Nietzsche, F. (1954). The Birth of Tragedy. In *The Philosophy of Nietzsche*. New York: Random House.
Nietzsche, F. (1976). On Truth and Lie in their Extra-Moral Sense. In *The Portable Nietzsche*, W. Kaufmann (Ed.), 45-47. New York: Penguin Books.
Nietzsche, F. (2006). *Thus spoke Zarathustra*. Del Caro and R. Pippin (Eds.). Cambridge, UK: Cambridge University Press.
Nitzsch, G. W. (1841). *Die Heldensage der Griechen nach ihrer nationalen Geltung*. Kiel.
Nitzsch, G. W. (1852). *Die Sagen poesie der Griechen kritisch dargestellt*. Braunschweig.
Onians, R. B. (1989). *The Origins of European Thought*. Cambridge, UK: Cambridge University Press.
Otto, W. (1981). *Dionysus, myth and cult*. (R. Palmer, Trans.). Dallas TX: Spring Publications. (Original work published 1933).
Ovid (1916). *Metamorphoses*. (F.J. Miller, Trans.). Cambridge, MA: Harvard University Press.
Page, D. (1966). *The Homeric Odyssey*. Oxford: Clarendon Press.
Parry, A. (1971). *The Making of Homeric Verse: The Collected Papers of Milman Parry*. Oxford: Oxford University Press.
Parry, M. & Lord, A. (1954). *Serbocroatian Heroic Songs*. Cambridge, MA: Harvard University Press.
Pestalozzi, H. (1945). *Die Achilleis als Quelle der Ilias*. Zurich.
Pindar (1997). *Pythian Odes*. (W.H. Race, Trans.). Cambridge, MA: Harvard University Press.
Plato (1973). *Platonis Opera*, E. Burnet (Ed.). Oxford: Oxford Univ. Press.
Richards, I. A. (1936). *The Philosophy of Rhetoric*. New York: Oxford University Press.
Richards, I. A. (1970). *Principles of Literary Criticism*. London: Routledge and Kegan Paul.
Ricoeur, P. (1975). *La métaphore vive*. Paris: Seuil.
Ricoeur, P. (1979). The Metaphorical Process as Cognition, Imagination, and Feeling. In *On Metaphor*, S. Sacks (Ed.), 141-157. Chicago, IL: University of Chicago Press.
Ricoeur, P. (1988). *Time and Narrative*, Vol. 3. Chicago, IL: University of Chicago Press.
Ridgeway, W. (1966). *The origin of tragedy*. New York: Benjamin Blom.

Rilke, R. M. (1982). *The Selected Poetry of Rainer Maria Rilke*. (S. Mitchell, Trans.). New York: Random House.
Rogers, R. (1978). *Metaphor, A Psychoanalytic View*. Berkeley, CA: University of California Press.
Rohde, E. (1893). *Psyche*. Heidelberg.
Schadewaldt, W. (1938). *Iliasstudien*. Leipsig.
Schadewaldt, W. (1965). *Von Homers Welt und Werk*. Stuttgard: K. F. Koehler Verlag.
Schadewaldt, W. (1966). Νέα κριτήρια γιά τήν ανάλυση της Οδύσσειας. In *Επιστροφή στήν Οδύσσεια*. Δ. Ιακώβ, Ι. Καζαζής, Α. Πηγάκος (Επιμελ.). Θεσσαλονίκη: Βανιάς, 1999.
Scheler, M. (1972). *On the eternal in man*. North Haven CT: Archon Books.
Schiller von F. (1943). *Lettres sur l'éducation esthétique de l'homme*. (R. Leroux, Trans.). Paris: Aubier, éditions Montaigne.
Schmitz, L.D. (2007). *Correspondence between Schiller and Goethe from 1794 to 1805*, v. 2. Whitefish, MT: Kessinger Publishing Company.
Scott, W. C. M. (1975). Remembering, Sleep and Dreams. *The International Review of Psycho-Analysis, 2*, 253-354.
Segal, H. (1957). Notes on symbol formation. *International Journal of Psycho-Analysis, 38*, 391-397.
Sharpe, E. F. (1950). Psycho-physical problems revealed in language: an examination of metaphor. In *Collected Papers on Psychoanalysis*, M. Brierley (Ed.), 155-169. London: Hogarth Press.
Shelley, P. B. (1965). A Defense of Poetry. In *The Complete Works of P. B. Shelley*, R. Ingpen & W. Peck (Ed.). New York: Gordian Press.
Sophokles (1981). *Antigone*. Cambridge, MA: Harvard University Press.
Steiner, G. (1996). *Antigones*. New Haven, CT: Yale University Press.
Tate, A. (Ed.) (1942). *The Language of Poetry*. Princeton, N.J.: Princeton University Press.
Verity, A. (2011). *The Iliad*. London: Oxford University press.
Vernant, J-P. (1996). *Mythe et pensée chez les Grecs*. Paris: La Découverte.
Virgil. (1935). *Georgics*. (H. R. Fairclough, Trans.). Cambridge, MA: Harvard University Press.
Virgil. (1984). *The Aeneid*. (R. Fitzerald, Trans.). New York: Vintage Books.
West, M. L. (2003). *Homeric Hymns. Homeric Apocrypha. Lives of Homer*. Cambridge, MA: Harvard University Press.
Whitaker, R. (2012). *The Iliad*. A South African Translation. Cape Town: New Voices.
Whitman, C. H. (1958). *Homer and the Heroic Tradition*. Cambridge, MA: Harvard University Press.
Wilamowitz-Möllendorf, von, U. (1884). *Homerische Untersuchungen*, Berlin.
Wilamowitz-Möllendorf, von, U. (1920). *Die Ilias und Homer*. Berlin.
Wilamowitz-Möllendorf, von, U. (1927). *Die Heimkehr des Odysseus*. Berlin.
Winnicott, D. W. (1958). *Collected Papers*. London: Tavistock Publications
Winnicott, D. W. (1965). *The Maturational Process and the Facilitating Environment*. London: Hogarth Press
Winnicott, D. W. (1971). *Playing and Reality*. London: Tavistock Publications.
Winnicott, D. W. (1975). The Depressive Position in Normal Emotional Development. In *Through Paediatrics to Psycho-Analysis*. London: Hogarth Press and the Institute of Psycho-Analysis.
Wittgenstein, L. (2009). *Philosophical Investigations*. G. E. M. Anscombe, P. M. S. Hacker, and J. Schulte, (Trans). West Sussex, UK: Wiley- Blackwell.

Wolf, F. A. (1985). *Prolegomena to Homer*. (A. Grafton, G.W.Most, & J. Zetzel, Ed. And Trans.). Princeton, NJ. (Original work published 1795).

www.ingramcontent.com/pod-product-compliance
Lightning Source LLC
Chambersburg PA
CBHW070629300426
44113CB00010B/1717